Bible Teaching for Preschoolers

Zadabeth Uland

Convention Press
Nashville, Tennessee

© Copyright 1984 • Convention Press
All rights reserved
5163-98
This book is the text
for Course number 13373 in the subject area
'Sunday School Leadership' of the Church Study Course.
Dewey Decimal Classification Number: 268.432
Subject Headings: SUNDAY SCHOOLS—PRESCHOOL CHILDREN //
RELIGIOUS EDUCATION OF PRESCHOOL CHILDREN
Printed in the United States of America.
Available from Baptist Book Stores.
Sunday School Department
The Sunday School Board of the Southern Baptist Convention
127 Ninth Avenue, North
Nashville, Tennessee 37234

ABOUT THE AUTHOR

Zadabeth Dupree Uland is an unforgettable Texan. She is a staff member at First Baptist Church in Plano, Texas, where she has served as minister of childhood education since the fall of 1970. Prior to joining the staff she had been serving in various capacities as a teacher of preschoolers, director of a preschool department, and as the coordinator of preschool programs. Having had nearly forty years of experience with preschoolers at First Baptist, she has had many opportunities to practice teaching preschoolers about the Bible.

Zadabeth Uland has written curriculum materials for Vacation Bible School, Backyard Bible Clubs, and *Preschool Bible Teacher C*. Her articles have been published in *Preschool Leadership* and *Living with Preschoolers*. She also authored *Things Families Do Together,* an undated unit for older preschoolers.

In addition to sharing with preschool teachers through her writings, she leads conferences for preschool teachers. She has shared through conferences at Ridgecrest and Glorieta Baptist Conference Centers and in numerous states. As part of the Bold Mission Thrust she accompanied others from First Baptist in mission work in Brazil.

Zadabeth and her husband Carl grew up in the church. They went to school, married, and reared a family there. Zadabeth and Carl, a retired egg producer and a trustee of Dallas Baptist College, enjoy traveling and antiquing. They also share an enthusiasm for football. They have two daughters, Trudy and Patty. Trudy is a kindergarten teacher and director in Arkansas. Patty is a physical therapist in Houston where she and her husband "Zip" Saxon live.

In Appreciation:

If there is help for you in reading this book, credit belongs not to me, but to God for his leadership in my life. Credit also belongs to the people and experiences that have been a part of my life.

I am especially grateful to:
- —my husband, Carl, who has always encouraged and supported the work I felt God calling me to do;

- —my daughters, Trudy and Patty, who gave me special insights into childhood and who now provide a source of fulfillment and joy to my life;

- —my parents, Clarice and Raymond Dupree, who provided a Christian home where love was felt;

- —my pastor, Travis Berry, who has helped me to understand the leadership of the Holy Spirit in our lives;

- —my fellow staff members, past and present, for helping me learn how to work with people;

- —my church for encouraging me to grow, develop, and learn, for providing the teaching of God's word in my life, and for allowing me to serve God in his way;

- —my long time teacher and supporter, Marion Armstrong, who started me on my path of working with preschoolers, and continues to help me in this work in our church;

- —Southern Baptists and to many special people at The Baptist Sunday School Board for opportunities of training and service far beyond anything I deserve;

- —all my friends over these years who have shared their lives, experiences, and knowledge to help me be a better teacher of preschoolers.

To each of these, I give my heartfelt gratitude.

Zadabeth Uland

Contents

INTRODUCTION 8
1. WHAT IS THE BIBLE? 9
2. THE KEY TO TEACHING PRESCHOOLERS THE BIBLE 39
3. THE DOOR TO TEACHING PRESCHOOLERS THE BIBLE 51
4. PLANNING TO TEACH PRESCHOOLERS THE BIBLE 67
5. REACHING PRESCHOOLERS TO TEACH 77
6. OPPORTUNITIES FOR TEACHING PRESCHOOLERS THE BIBLE 87
7. WORKING WITH OTHERS 97
8. THE REWARDS OF TEACHING 103
PERSONAL LEARNING ACTIVITIES 109
APPENDIX 118
   Bible Teaching Tools 118
   Bible Verses and Thoughts 145
   Resources 154
CHURCH STUDY COURSE INFORMATION 157

Introduction

This book, *Bible Teaching for Preschoolers,* is the product of the crucible of experience. Its author, Zadabeth Uland, has written these pages from her struggles related to the challenges encountered in teaching preschoolers the Bible. She has served for thirteen years on a church staff where her responsibilities relate to ministering to young children and their families. This book is, therefore, very practical and useable.

Bible Teaching for Preschoolers focuses on one major question: "How can we effectively teach preschoolers the Bible?" Each chapter is designed to answer this question from a variety of perspectives. For example, such areas as the teacher's concept of what the Bible is, planning, and reaching preschoolers and their families are given attention in this coordinated plan to show what is involved in teaching preschoolers the Bible.

I am deeply impressed with the content of this book. As preschool teachers, *Bible Teaching for Preschoolers* focuses on the essence of our work in practical, helpful terms. I am grateful that I have the opportunity to recommend such a splendid piece of work to you.

May your commitment to your calling as a preschool teacher be renewed and may you find practical help for your task as you read these pages.

Cos Davis, Supervisor
Preschool Program Section

Chapter 1
What Is the Bible?

The answer to the above question has been beautifully written numerous times by many theologians and scholars, as well as others. It is not possible for this writer to write anything that has not already been written in answer to the question. However, please let me, as a teacher of preschoolers, attempt to answer this question for myself and, perhaps, for other preschool teachers.

The Bible is the book of all books, comparable to no other. It is the book known and read by more people than any other book. A copy of the Bible may be found in more homes throughout the world than any other book. The Bible is the book most often given as a gift among families and friends. Without a doubt, the Bible has been printed in more languages than has any other book.

The Bible is a collection of books written by men inspired by the Holy Spirit. These books, written over a period of some fifteen hundred years, were written at different times and under a variety of circumstances. Yet, when read, the Bible has a message for people today.

The alarming factor in these statements attesting to the popularity of the Bible is that this book is often unused, unread, and unheeded by today's world. The mere presence of this book in a home does not assure more than that there is a significance in the presence of the book.

"The Holy Bible was written by men divinely inspired and is the record of God's revelation of Himself to man," according to the *Baptist Faith and Message*.[1] It has truth for its content and salvation and eternal life as a goal for each reader. It is a book of instruction and serves as a guide by which all Christians strive to live.

The Bible reveals the life of Jesus Christ who offers hope to the world, and grace, faith, peace, and comfort to the believer.

To understand what the Bible is, is only the beginning for the Christian. The endless treasure within this book has never been totally discovered. The *trail* or *map* to discovering the treasure is to:

    READ
            STUDY
                    INTERPRET
                            APPLY
                                    SHARE

This trail or map is available to all who will use it. It is necessary for the person who has been chosen to teach preschoolers. Before the Bible can be the textbook for the teacher, it must be the guidebook for the life of the teacher.

The Bible Is a Book for Preschool Teachers

            "He that would dare to teach
            must never cease to learn."
                      Benjamin Franklin

It has been said that we cannot teach what we do not know. Therefore, if we are to teach the Bible, teachers must, at times, become the learners. We must constantly seek to study and understand the Scriptures. Why is this so important if we are going to teach children in the preschool years?

1. I am a Christian and want to learn all I possibly can from God's Word.
2. I love God and want to please him by obeying his Word; I will use every means at my disposal to learn, from the Bible and from other books, what this book is saying to me.
3. I am a brother or sister of Jesus Christ, I want to learn all I can possibly learn about him and his example for my life.
4. I have been chosen by God and by my church to teach little children. I want to study the Bible so that I can model its meaning to them and help them apply its message to their daily lives.
5. At times I am so weak, I must have God's Word within my mind, heart, and soul as it gives me strength for every need and encouragement through every problem.
6. The Bible tells me how to live and the examples of important people in the lives of preschoolers is one of the best ways they can learn from the Bible.

Add your own thoughts as to why it is important for you to study the Bible. _____

_____

_____

There is no legitimate excuse not to read and study the Bible today. The Bible is accessible on tapes for those who, for various reasons, cannot read. It is printed in braille for those who cannot see. Many good translations, including several in today's language, are available to help us better understand the Scriptures. Bible studies are more popular than ever before. Most churches, in addition to the Bible study hour on Sunday morning, provide special times for study of the Scriptures. One need only inquire about when these special times are provided. In many churches, the Wednesday evening prayer service is an excellent opportunity to increase one's understanding of the Scriptures.

Thousands of books have been written to help people better understand the Scriptures. These books usually are written from one person's perspective and should be read with that in mind. As the Christian reads a book explaining the message of the Bible, a healthy reaction may occur. Mr. or Mrs. "Average" may not agree with the author, and hopefully will go to the Scriptures or to other books as a follow-up in his or her study.

Did you ever notice how excited you get when reading that with which you agree? It is encouraging to know that others think as we think. It is stimulating to read that which causes us to question. It is alright to question. It is good to question. As teachers, we must acknowledge that children learn through their curiosity. Hopefully, the more the teacher reads and studies God's Word, the more curious he will become about this Word and its importance to his life.

Perhaps Miss Bessie Wright, minister to children at Broadway Baptist Church, Fort Worth, Texas, for many years, best summed up what I am trying to say. As she concluded a Bible study she had been asked to bring to a group of preschool teachers, Bess Wright said, "I hope that you will all be people of one Book, but that does not mean you will not have many others."

Teachers, the Bible is a book for you. The more you read and study it, the more knowledgeable you will become. It is your guidebook for daily living. It is your textbook as you seek to guide preschoolers to learn from it.

A portion of a poem I have shared with many preschool teachers includes a statement by Antonio Stradivari, the great maker of violins. The poem states that Stradivari made violins rather than played them. Stradivari, in response to this statement, said that when the master violinist plays a violin he has made, he will be glad that Antonio Stradivari lived, made violins, and made them better than any other person could make them. Stradivari, in the poem, explained that God gives men the skill to play the violin and he (Stradivari) gives them the violin. Thus, God has chosen Stradivari to help him. Antonio poses the question of his failing to do his job and "robbing God." There would be no Stradivari violins without Antonio Stradivari. "'Tis God gives skill, but not without men's hands," according to Stradivari.

Just as God chose Antonio Stradivari to help him by making violins better than any other, he has chosen you to help him in a special way. God cannot teach the Bible to preschoolers in your church except through you. The responsibility is yours.

"And that from a child thou hast known the holy scriptures, which are able to make thee wise unto salvation through faith which is in Christ Jesus. All scripture is given by inspiration of God, and is profitable for doctrine, for reproof, for correction, for instruction in righteousness:
That the man of God may be perfect, thoroughly furnished unto all good works."

2 Timothy 3:15-17

The Bible Is a Book for Preschoolers

Two- and one-half-year-old Julie moved ahead of her parents and almost ran into her room at church. Greeted by Mrs. Scott, Julie, with eyes sparkling, said, "Look at my Bible," as she handed her new Bible to her teacher. "I like your Bible, Julie," said Mrs. Scott. "Tell me about it," she added. "It is my Bible. My Grandma sent it to me." With these two statements, Julie gave the information she was capable of giving verbally about the Bible. As people interested in preschoolers, it is important for us to be aware of other ways Julie has been and was being affected and influenced in her knowledge and feelings about the Bible.

Perhaps from the time of infancy, Julie had observed her parents, teachers, or other adults carefully handling the Bible. Hopefully, as she came to her room at church each week, she heard her teachers talk about the Bible and her attention was captured by the pictures she was shown. Possibly in her family, living in a Christian home, Julie observed her parents' use of the Bible in a family devotion time. Julie was aware of other members of the family having a personal Bible and bringing their Bibles to church. Already Julie has developed attitudes and feelings about the Bible that will remain throughout her life.

Five-year-old Todd came to Vacation Bible School with his neighbors who are church members. Todd did not attend a church regularly. Each day Todd heard Bible stories. Teachers showed Todd where, in the department Bible, stories, verses, and thoughts, were located. Todd's response, "I wish I had a Bible," made the teachers aware of Todd's impression of this book and of his desire to learn more from it.

How do we know that the Bible is a book for preschoolers? We find within its message the answer to our question. Isaiah 54:13 says, "All thy children shall be taught of the Lord; and great shall be the peace of thy children." Isaiah 40:11 says, ". . . he shall gather the lambs with his arm, and carry them in his bosom, ..." Matthew 18:4-5 says, "Whosoever therefore shall humble himself as this little child, the same is the greatest in the kingdom of heaven. And whoso shall receive one such little child in my name receiveth me." Matthew 19:14 gives an account of Jesus' words, ". . . Suffer little children, and forbid them not, to come unto me: for of such is the kingdom of heaven." Again and again the Scriptures emphasize the importance of children in the sight of God. They leave no question as to whether his Word is for children as well as for adults.

One of the strongest statements about children and the Scriptures is found in Deuteronomy 6:4-7: "Hear, O Israel: The Lord our God is one Lord: And thou shalt love the Lord thy God with all thine heart, and with all thy soul, and with all thy might. And these words, which I command thee this day, shall be in thine heart: And thou shalt teach them diligently unto thy children, and shalt talk of them when thou sittest in thine house, and when thou walkest by the way, and when thou liest down, and when thou risest up." This directive leaves no doubt about teaching children Bible truths. Therefore, if the Bible is a book for preschoolers, God has a plan to help them understand its message. That plan includes:

    YOU, THE TEACHER
      YOU, THE PARENT
        YOU, THE CHURCH

"We love the Bible;
We love its stories true;
The Bible tells of Jesus
And that he loves us, too."[2]

Twelve five-year-olds and their teachers sang this song as they sat in a semicircle in a preschool room on Sunday morning. As they finished, the director gently opened the Bible on her lap and began to tell the story "Jesus and the Children." The children listened as if hearing this story for the first time. As the director came to the climax, she told how Jesus' helpers wanted to send the children away. Then she said, "Jesus heard his helpers and he said, 'Do not send the children away. Bring them here to me. I love all the children.'" The group sat quietly for a moment before one child said, "I like that story." The director quickly responded, with "I think we all like that story. Let's say thank you to God for the Bible that tells us about Jesus."

Yes, the Bible is for preschoolers. Their love and appreciation for this book will be greatly determined by the example, attitudes, and teachings of important adults in their lives. What preschoolers learn from the Bible and about the Bible will be taught to them by teachers and parents. Because it is written in adult language, the Bible must be interpreted to young children.

What is the Bible to preschoolers? It is what you, the child's teacher, feel yourself and what you guide the child to feel about it. To guide the child in learning from the Bible means that the teacher must have:
1. An understanding of the Scriptures.
2. An understanding of preschoolers and how they learn.
3. A goal or objective for preschoolers in their most formative years.

Objectives for Teaching Preschoolers

A teacher must have a goal or objective so that he or she may formulate strategies and plans to move the learner toward that objective. The objectives a church has for preschoolers should help lay a spiritual foundation for the life of each child. The tasks of the church are to reach, teach, win, and develop. Preschoolers are not considered to be of the age of accountability; however, the ultimate goal for every child is that someday he will choose Jesus Christ as his personal Savior. Therefore, three of the four tasks are applicable for teachers to use with preschoolers. Perhaps overall goals may be stated this way:

- Reach each preschooler and his family for Bible study.
- Enrich the present spiritual growth of each child.
- Lay foundations for conversion when a child reaches the age of accountability.
- Provide guidance and opportunities that will help each preschooler develop into a responsible Christian and church member after conversion.

Obviously these objectives are very general in nature and must be applied according to the maturity level of the learner. Specific helps for the teacher are available in the teaching guides for each age group and in other church study course books. *Understanding Today's Preschoolers* and *How to Guide Preschoolers* are two books that preschool teachers will find especially helpful.

Laying a Basic Spiritual Foundation
Just as the teacher needs help from books and from other persons in interpreting the Bible, the preschooler needs even more help in understanding and applying of the Scriptures.

Preschoolers must be taught at their level and with methods through which they learn best. The normal child is developing:
MENTALLY
PHYSICALLY
EMOTIONALLY
SOCIALLY
SPIRITUALLY

This development is occurring simultaneously in most preschoolers. Specific needs in one or more areas may be evident in some preschoolers. Preschool teachers need to be alert to these needs and strive to help preschoolers develop equally in each one.

Four-year-old Wes came to Sunday School every Sunday. He would choose a quiet activity and play alone, occasionally talking with his teachers. If science materials such as magnets or batteries that ring bells were provided, Wes was especially interested. His explanation of how these things worked astounded his teachers. A teacher opened the door to the air conditioning unit one day and Wes surprised her by knowing about that machinery just as he knew about magnets and batteries. But Wes never joined in play with other boys and girls. He was a brilliant child who had not learned how to relate to other children his age. He was not an especially happy child because of his lack of social development. A child needs to develop equally if he is to feel good about himself and to learn to trust other people. Preschool teachers can help to encourage this total development. Study chapter 1 of the book *Understanding Today's Preschoolers* by C. Sybil Waldrop, to help you better understand the preschooler at each age level and in each developmental stage.

Eight Subject Areas

Based on what is known about how preschoolers develop and what they are capable of learning, eight subject areas are used to teach preschoolers as much as they are capable of learning about the Bible.

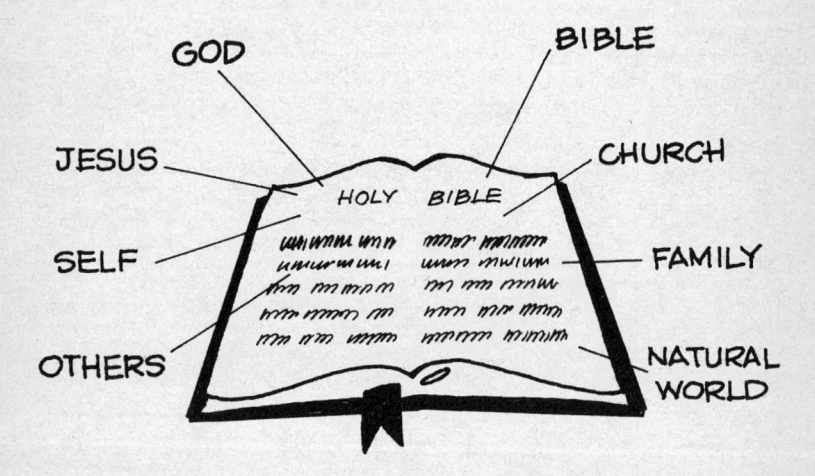

Teaching objectives for each of these subject or scope areas are defined in each unit of study for preschoolers. The teaching objectives for each subject or scope area are identified in the *Church Curriculum Base Design* notebook. This information is used by those who write and edit preschool curriculum. It is hoped that by sharing a portion of that information here, teachers may be encouraged to better understand how the objectives relate to the subject (or scope) areas. This information is to help preschool teachers become more aware of opportunities they have to develop spiritual attitudes and concepts and to instill biblical truths in preschoolers they teach. Teachers may find it helpful, also, to give attention to the progression of learning for the different age levels.

PRESCHOOL TEACHING OBJECTIVES AS RELATED TO SCOPE (OR SUBJECT) AREAS

BABIES, CREEPERS, TODDLERS

SCOPE	OBJECTIVES
GOD God is a name.	• To provide opportunities for each child to hear God's name • To help each child have positive feelings when he hears God's name
God is a person.	• To help each child hear about ways that God is good to him • To provide opportunities for each child to hear the words *God loves you* • To provide opportunities for each child to hear teachers say, "Thank you, God"
NATURAL WORLD God made things I can explore with my senses.	• To provide opportunities for each child to see, hear, and touch things God made
God made the animals.	• To provide opportunities for preschoolers to see a variety of animals and hear that God made the animals
God made things I can discover.	• To help preschoolers make discoveries in their world
JESUS Jesus is a name.	• To provide opportunities for each child to hear the name of Jesus • To help each child have positive feelings when he hears Jesus' name

SCOPE	OBJECTIVES
Jesus is a person.	• To provide opportunities for each child to hear the words *Jesus loves you* • To help each child see pictures of and hear about Jesus as a child • To help each child see pictures of and hear about Jesus as a man • To provide opportunities for each child to hear how Jesus helped others • To help each child have a growing awareness that Jesus is a special person
Easter is a special day.	• To provide opportunities for each child to hear about Easter as a special day (focus statement for one session) • To provide opportunities for each child to hear the words *Jesus loves you*
SELF I am a person.	• To help each child sense that he is special and important because God made him • To provide opportunities for the child to hear that God made him, God made him to grow, God gave him (hands) (to push the ball) • To provide opportunities for each child to be aware of things God planned for him to do • To provide opportunities for each child to be more aware of the body God made for him

SCOPE	OBJECTIVES
	• To provide opportunities for each preschooler to make appropriate choices as he uses his senses that God gave him
FAMILY I have a family.	• To provide opportunities for preschoolers to become aware that God made families • To provide opportunities for each child to hear about ways Christian family members show their love • To help each child associate warm feelings with his family
CHURCH People at church love me.	• To provide opportunities for each child to become aware of people at church • To help each child feel secure with people at church • To help each child feel secure in his room at church • To help each child enjoy being at church
People take care of me at the church building.	• To provide opportunities for preschoolers to become aware of people at the church building who care for them
I use books, pictures, toys, and puzzles at church.	• To provide opportunities for each child to enjoy a variety of learning activities at church
People at church talk and sing about God and Jesus.	• To provide opportunities for each child to hear teachers talk and sing about God and Jesus

SCOPE	OBJECTIVES
BIBLE The Bible is a book. The Bible is a special book (older toddlers).	• To provide opportunities for each child to see and touch the Bible
I hear about Jesus when the Bible is used.	• To provide opportunities for each child to hear about Jesus when a teacher uses the Bible
OTHERS People love me.	• To help each child become aware that people love him
People take care of my needs.	• To help each child become aware that people take care of his needs
I am aware of other people.	• To help the child have a growing awareness of people around him • To help the child enjoy being with other people

TWOS AND THREES

SCOPE	OBJECTIVES
GOD God made people.	• To help the child become aware that God made him and others
God loves people. God is a person.	• To provide opportunities for the child to hear God's name • To provide opportunities for each child to hear that God loves him • To provide opportunities for each child to become more aware of ways God shows his love for all people
God wants people to love him.	• To help each child become more aware of ways people show their love for God

SCOPE	OBJECTIVES
People talk to God.	• To help each child express thanks to God • To provide opportunities for each child to hear his teachers talk to God • To provide opportunities for each child to talk to God
God wants people to love and help each other.	• To provide opportunities for each child to hear about ways people help each other • To provide opportunities for each child to help others
God made plants and animals.	• To provide opportunities for each child to become aware that God made plants and animals • To provide opportunities for each child to discover and explore things God made • To provide opportunities for each child to help take care of plants and animals
God made earth and sky.	• To help the child be aware that God made the world
NATURAL WORLD God provided food for people and animals. God made people. God made plants and animals. God made earth and sky.	• To provide opportunities for twos and threes to hear about the animals God made • To help twos and threes associate God's name with natural wonders • To help twos and threes discover the world God made • To help children be aware of the things God made

SCOPE	OBJECTIVES
JESUS Jesus was born.	• To provide opportunities for each child to associate the events surrounding the birth of Jesus with feelings of love and happiness • To provide opportunities for each child to associate the birth of Jesus with Christmas
Jesus loves people.	• To provide opportunities for each child to hear that Jesus loves him and other people • To help each child hear about ways Jesus showed his love for people
Jesus wants people to love him.	• To provide opportunities for each child to hear about people in the Bible who loved Jesus • To provide opportunities for each child to hear about people today who love Jesus
Jesus had a family.	• To help each child become more aware that Jesus had a family
Jesus helped people.	• To provide opportunities for each child to hear about ways Jesus helped people
Jesus grew.	• To provide opportunities for each child to become more aware that Baby Jesus grew • To provide opportunities for each child to hear about Jesus as a baby and young boy
Jesus wants people to love and help each other.	• To provide opportunities for each child to hear about ways people help each other

SCOPE	OBJECTIVES
	• To provide opportunities for each child to help others
Easter is a special day.	• To provide opportunities for the child to hear about Easter as a special time to think about Jesus
SELF I am an important person.	• To provide opportunities for twos and threes to discover ways that they are important to other people • To provide opportunities for twos and threes to be more aware that God loves them • To provide opportunities for twos and threes to be more aware that people around them love and accept them • To provide opportunities for each child to become aware that God made each person special and different • To provide opportunities for the child to hear about Easter as a special time to think about Jesus
I can do many things.	• To help each child associate God with his ability to do things
I am growing.	• To provide opportunities for each child to become more aware that God helps him grow • To help each child become aware that God wants each person to grow

SCOPE	OBJECTIVES
FAMILY Other people are in my family.	• To provide opportunities for each child to feel that he is an important person in his family
My family loves me.	• To help each child feel loved and wanted by his family • To help each child feel happy to be a part of a family that loves one another and works together
Family members help one another.	• To provide opportunities for each child to hear about ways families love and work together
I can help my family.	• To help each child become aware of ways he helps his family • To provide opportunities for each child to talk about ways he can help in his family
God planned for families.	• To provide opportunities for each child to become aware that God planned for families • To help each child become aware that being in a family is God's plan for people
CHURCH I know other children and adults at church.	• To provide opportunities for each child to become more aware of friends at church who love him • To provide opportunities for each child to feel happy and secure with church friends • To provide opportunities for each child to feel he is an important person at church

SCOPE	OBJECTIVES
People at church talk about God and Jesus.	• To provide opportunities for each child to hear stories about Bible people who enjoyed being at church • To provide opportunities for each child to hear about God and Jesus
I can help at church.	• To help each child become more aware of ways he can help at church • To provide opportunities for each child to help at church • To help each child become aware that stories in the Bible tell about people who helped at church
People at church help others.	• To provide opportunities for each child to identify ways people at church help others
BIBLE The Bible is a book about God and Jesus.	• To provide opportunities for each child to develop in his understanding that the Bible is about God and Jesus
The Bible has stories and verses about God, Jesus, and people.	• To help each child develop his awareness that the Bible is a book with stories about people • To help each child have an increased desire to hear stories about people in the Bible
OTHERS Other people to help me.	• To help each child identify ways people help him
I can love and help others.	• To help each child identify ways he can help others

SCOPE	OBJECTIVES
	• To provide opportunities for each child to discover ways that he can be kind and loving to others
Others love me and care about me.	• To provide opportunities for each child to select ways that he will be kind and loving to others

FOURS AND FIVES

SCOPE	OBJECTIVES
GOD God loves and cares for people.	• To help the child become more aware that God loves people and wants people to love him • To help each child develop more understanding that God provides and cares for people
God can do things that people cannot do.	• To provide opportunities for each child to develop increased awareness that God can do things that people cannot do
God wants people to worship him.	• To provide opportunities for each child to become more aware that God wants people to worship him (read the Bible, sing, pray)
God wants people to talk to him.	• To help each child become more aware that he can talk to God anytime and anyplace • To help each child become aware that God hears our prayers anytime
God wants people to thank him.	• To provide opportunities for each child to thank God for his love and care

SCOPE	OBJECTIVES
God wants people everywhere to learn about him.	• To provide opportunities for each child to become more aware that God wants people to learn about him
NATURAL WORLD God made people, animals, plants, and things in the natural world. • God made earth and sky. • God made rain, snow, and wind. • God made day and night. • God made sun, moon, and stars.	• To help the child become more aware that God showed his love by making people and things in the natural world
God wants people, animals, and plants to grow.	• To help the child become more aware that God wants people, animals, and plants to grow
God wants people to care for the things he made.	• To help the child become more aware that things God made need care • To help the child become more aware of how he can take care of things God made
JESUS Jesus is God's Son. (basic to Easter session)	• To help each child develop more awareness that God showed his love by sending his Son, Jesus • To provide opportunities for each child to hear that Jesus is God's Son
Jesus loves me and other people.	• To help each child become more aware that Jesus loves and helps him

SCOPE	OBJECTIVES
	• To help the child develop more awareness that Jesus loves all people • To provide opportunities for each child to become more aware of Jesus' love for other people
Jesus was born. Jesus was a baby.	• To help the child become more aware of the events surrounding the birth of Jesus
Jesus was a boy.	• To help each child develop more awareness that Jesus grew to be a boy
Jesus was a man.	• To help each child develop more awareness that Jesus grew to be a man
Jesus helped people because he loved them.	• To help each child develop more understanding that Jesus helped people because he loved them • To help the child develop more awareness that Jesus helped people who needed his help
Jesus can do things that people cannot do.	• To help each child become more aware of things Jesus can do that we cannot do
Jesus had a family.	
Jesus wants people to love him.	• To help the child become more aware that Jesus wants people to love him
Jesus grew from a baby to a man.	• To help fours and fives develop more awareness that Jesus grew from a baby to a man

SCOPE	OBJECTIVES
SELF I am important to God, self, and others.	• To help each child become more aware that he is important because God made him • To help each child become more aware that he is of worth to himself, others, and God
I can think, work, and play because God gave me abilities.	• To help each child express his feelings, attitudes, and actions in increasingly positive ways • To help each child become more aware that he can do many things • To help each child develop more understanding that God gives each person the ability to learn and to work
I can make some choices.	• To provide opportunities for each child to make appropriate choices
God wants me to take care of my body.	• To help each child become aware of ways that God wants him to take care of his body
I am growing as God planned for me to grow.	• To help each child develop more awareness that God wants each person to grow • To help each child develop more understanding that God wants each person to use his mind and his body
I can take turns and share.	• To provide opportunities for each child to take turns and share with others
FAMILY I am a member of a family.	• To help each child become increasingly aware that he belongs to a family

SCOPE	OBJECTIVES
Each family member has his own belongings and tasks to do.	• To help each child become more aware that each family member has his own belongings and tasks to do
My family loves me.	
Family members help one another.	• To help the child become more aware of ways members of his family help him
I can help my family.	• To help the child become aware of ways he can help at home
God wants people to live together in families.	• To help each child become more aware that God wants people to live together in families
God wants people to work together in families.	• To help each child become aware that God wants people to work together in families
God wants people to play together in families.	• To help each child become aware that God wants people to play together as families
The Bible has stories about families who helped one another.	• To help each child develop more awareness that the Bible has stories about how families help each other
BIBLE The Bible is an important book.	• To provide opportunities for each child to develop more awareness that the Bible is more important than any other book • To help each child know some Bible stories and Bible thoughts and verses

SCOPE	OBJECTIVES
The Bible helps people know how God wants them to live.	• To help each child become more aware that the Bible is a book that helps people know how God wants them to live • To give each child opportunities to hear Bible stories and Bible verses and thoughts that tell people how to treat other people • To help each child become more aware that Bible truths relate to his everyday life
The Bible has stories about how people have shown their love for God and Jesus.	• To provide opportunities for each child to hear about ways people in the Bible have shown their love for God and Jesus
The Bible has stories and verses that tell about God, Jesus, and people.	• To help each child hear Bible stories and Bible thoughts and verses about God and Jesus • To provide opportunities for each child to hear Bible stories and Bible verses and thoughts about how people worked together
The Bible has stories about things Jesus did.	• To help each child become more aware that the Bible tells how Jesus helped people • To help the child become more aware that the Bible has stories about the things Jesus did
OTHERS Certain people love and help me.	• To help the child develop more understanding that there are people who love and help him

SCOPE	OBJECTIVES
	• To help each child become aware of ways to say thank you to those who help him
I can love and help others in many ways.	• To help each child think of ways God wants him to help others
I can be considerate of others' rights and feelings.	• To help each child become more aware that each person has some rights and feelings
Each person has tasks to do.	• To help each child become more aware that each person has tasks to do
People are alike in some ways and different in some ways.	• To help the child become more aware that God made people alike in some ways and different in some ways
God wants people to love and help each other.	• To help each child become more aware that God wants people to love and help others
Jesus wants people to love and help each other.	• To help each child become more aware that God wants people to love and help others
Some things belong to me and some things belong to others.	• To help the child develop more understanding that some things belong to him and some things belong to others
People have different kinds of work to do.	• To provide opportunities for each child to become aware that God wants people to work • To help each child develop more understanding that God gives each person the ability to learn and to work

SCOPE	OBJECTIVES
	• To help the child develop more awareness of people at home and at church who help him
God wants people to be friendly and have friends.	• To help each child develop more awareness that God wants people to be kind to other people • To help each child become more aware of what it means to be a friend
CHURCH At church, people sing songs, listen to Bible stories, and talk about God and Jesus.	• To help each child develop more awareness that people at church sing, pray, and read the Bible together • To help each child develop more awareness that churches are a part of what God wants for people
I can be a helper at church.	• To help each child discover ways he can help at church
People use the Bible at church.	• To provide opportunities for each child to develop more awareness of ways the Bible is used at church
People at church have different tasks to do.	• To help each child become more aware that people at church have many kinds of work to do • To help the child become more aware that people at church work together to tell others about God and Jesus
People give money at church.	• To help the child develop more understanding that giving money at church helps buy the things he uses at church

SCOPE	OBJECTIVES
People go to different church buildings.	• To provide opportunities for each child to develop more awareness that people go to different churches
People at church help people who need help.	• To help each child become more aware of the ways a church helps people who need help • To help each child become more aware that at church there are people who love God and want to help others
People at church love and care for me.	• To help the child become more aware that people at church help one another
Going to church is important.	• To help each child become more aware that going to church is important
I have friends at church.	• To provide opportunities for each child to become more aware of his friends at church

Concepts, Attitudes, and Feelings

Learning begins before a child is born. The unborn baby reacts to sounds as he moves to loud noises or calms to music. He learns about his family as he hears them talk before his birth. From infancy, young children are developing concepts, attitudes, and feelings. These, plus facts and information they receive and assimilate, become a part of their storehouse of knowledge and will affect their total life.

Elizabeth and Deborah are twin girls born into a Christian home. They have been in church since they were three weeks old. Their parents love God and support the church. On their way to church Elizabeth and Deborah hear their parents use terms such as Jesus, God, and church. "Good morning, Elizabeth. Good morning, Deborah. How are my girls?" Mrs.

Roberts may ask as the twins arrive in their room. As a teacher changes Deborah's diaper, she sings: "I am happy, I am happy. Deborah is here today."[3] Mrs. Carol, feeding Elizabeth, says: "Thank you, God, for Elizabeth. Thank you for good milk to drink."

Kimberly has just started walking. A smile on her face and her movement about the room indicate that she is happy and secure in her room at church. Her teacher sings: "Jesus, Jesus, I love Jesus. Jesus, Jesus, he loves Kimberly."[4] Babies, creepers, and toddlers are developing important concepts, feelings, and attitudes about the church, the Bible, God, Jesus, and other people as they have these kinds of learning experiences at church. Yes, even at this age, teaching has begun and learning is taking place.

We often use the terms *feelings, attitudes,* and *concepts*. Definitions of these terms are easily obtained from any dictionary. Describing the difference in them is difficult. These words are not the same, but because of the ultimate effect they have on the human being, they are very closely related. *Concept* may be defined as an idea, a thought, or something created in one's mind. *Attitude* involves one's disposition or opinion. It is a mental position. The term *feeling*, as we are using it here, means an awareness, consciousness, opinion, or belief. These inner avenues of learning affects the way a child feels toward God, Jesus, his church, himself, and other people for the rest of his life.

As the child is made more comfortable physically with a diaper change, he hears terms such as *God, Jesus, church,* and *love* and he associates these with a warm, comfortable feeling. As a baby is given a bottle and a teacher says, "Thank you, God, for Elizabeth," she can associate these words with a feeling of security and satisfaction.

Mrs. Posey opens the Bible to the story of David. Two-year-old Nikki moves close. The story, perhaps six lines, is about how David was a helper. Nikki may sense that what David did pleased David's father and that Mrs. Posey, whom she loves, approves too.

Three-year-old Michael is hammering with the toy hammer in the block area. His teacher comments, "Jesus learned how to use a hammer when he was a boy, Michael. Jesus helped Joseph hammer and saw in the carpenter shop." Michael may not stop hammering but his three-year-old mind has absorbed a fact that he will recall later.

In the five-year department, the director introduces a game.

"I will begin a story from the Bible. Raise your hand if you know the name of the person in the story." The boys and girls know the answers to almost every story. This has occurred as a gradual learning process. Visible results such as this are exciting and rewarding to teachers. Names and facts are important. Perhaps what is most important is that the children are experiencing happy times associated with significant persons using the Bible. Young children can learn facts, but they may not understand them. Understanding the Bible comes from a practical application of biblical information in the life of the child. Feelings, attitudes, and concepts are developed as a result of experiences with appropriate materials, with adults, or with other children.

These experiences at church and other experiences children have at home are ways adults help instill a basic spiritual foundation in the lives of preschoolers.

The best opportunities to teach preschoolers are those that occur out of natural or everyday situations. Helping preschool teachers to be alert to these opportunities and be prepared to use them is part of what this book is intended to do. The challenge of being alert to teaching opportunities or of creating teaching opportunities is exciting. It means, for the teacher, thorough preparation for each session. It means not just collecting necessary materials, but thinking ahead of time about how the Bible teaching aim may be accomplished in each session.

Self-Worth

One other aspect of foundational teaching is the importance of the child's feeling of self-worth. From infancy, the struggle to be individual is evident. This is a natural desire and is as God planned. God did not make any two of us alike. Even identical twins have some distinguishing mark and have differing personalities. Each person deserves to be himself—to feel that he is a person of worth. A noted child specialist once wrote that the goal of selfhood was dependent upon the child's achievement of self-esteem. This self-esteem is either encouraged or discouraged by the important adults in the life of each child.

The child senses in adults their attitudes toward him. He often responds as a result of this feeling. Teachers need to feel that each child is unique, that each is important, and that each one is depending on adults in his life to help him develop a positive feeling of self-worth. This positive feeling of self-worth can be the motivating factor behind the child's confidence in himself and others, his eagerness to explore and learn, and his response to the world about him.

One of our ultimate goals is to lay foundations for conversion when the child reaches the age of accountability. (Use of the term "age of accountability" indicates accountability to God.) This level of understanding is usually reached during preadolescence. As preschool teachers, our job is to lay the foundation. It will be valuable for a child to feel that he has worth and for him to experience the love of other human beings before he can be expected to believe that Jesus could love him so much that he would die for his sins. Although this experience comes beyond preschool years, laying the foundation includes encouraging the child's feeling of self-worth. Therefore, ways that teachers can help a child develop a better self-concept may be some of the most important teaching they can do. In other words, teaching that encourages preschoolers to feel worthwhile is as biblically sound as the Bible facts and information some would label as "teaching the Bible."

Teachers may encourage a feeling of self-worth in preschoolers in many ways. Some ways of encouraging self-worth include:

Learning and using the child's name.
Visiting in the child's home.
Regular attendance by the teacher.
Cuddling the infant and singing to her.
Responding to the cry of a baby.
Listening when a child wants to tell you something.
Encouraging the child to do all for himself that he is capable of doing.
Praising a child's efforts to develop skills and to learn.
Commending a child's acceptable behavior.
Providing various activities through which a child may experience success.
Being in the room when the first child arrives.
Planning activities that can motivate and challenge preschoolers to learn.
Add your suggestions to the list.

_____

_____

_____

_____

[1] *Baptist Faith and Message.* (Nashville: The Sunday School Board of the Southern Baptist Convention, 1963), p. 7.
[2] Words and Music by Marie Ingham © Copyright 1959 The Sunday School Board of the Southern Baptist Convention. All rights reserved. Used by permission.
[3] Tune "I Am Happy," *Songs for the Young Child.* p. 38.
[4] Tune "Jesus, Jesus," *Songs for the Young Child.* p. 16.

Chapter 2
The Key to Teaching Preschoolers the Bible

"Having then gifts differing according to the grace that is given to us, whether prophecy, let us prophesy according to the proportion of faith; Or ministry, let us wait on our ministering: or he that teacheth on teaching; Or he that exhorteth, on exhortation: he that giveth, let him do it with simplicity; he that ruleth, with diligence; he that showeth mercy, with cheerfulness." Romans 12:6-18.

The Teacher Is the Key
I wish I had the gift of writing poetry, or singing, or playing a musical instrument. I wish I could paint a beautiful picture or sew a beautiful garment. I can do none of these things, yet God has given to me special gifts just as he has given special gifts to you. These gifts are not always what we would choose, nor are they always evident. It is my belief that these gifts surface most often as one opens his or her life to whatever God has for him to do.

Having prayed before approaching a prospective teacher, I felt confident as I asked her about the possibility of teaching in a department of three-year-olds. Her answer was, "I'll pray about it to see if it is where God wants me to be." This seemed a logical answer, I said I would contact her again by the end of the week. My next prospective teacher was a young father. I had observed his consistent attendance and the sincerity of his Christian commitment. His answer was, "I had not thought about teaching five-year-olds, however, if this is where I am needed, I will do my best." His response prompted some thoughts. Here is a Christian ready to serve wherever he is needed. What better direction from God as to his will for one's life than to be approached about a teaching position that is open. For some reason, your name was put into the mind of the person approaching you. This person, too, may be led by God to you.

Accepting a responsibility of teaching young children is an awesome task. It should be accepted and approached with prayer. It is one of the most important jobs a person will ever perform. It would be much easier to sit in an adult class, but you have been chosen by your church and by God. The kind of teacher you become is up to you.

Responsibilities from God

Through his word, God has given some important responsibilities to preschool teachers:

To Pray

"Let hope keep you joyful; in trouble stand firm, persist in prayer" (Rom. 12:12, NEB).[1] Staying in close communication with God means listening as well as talking. A teacher will want to be open to the Holy Spirit as he or she seeks to guide boys and girls in learning about God's love expressed through his Son, through other people, and through the natural world. A purposeful prayer life is vital to any Christian and is necessary for every teacher.

To Study

"Study to shew thyself approved unto God, a workman that needeth not to be ashamed, rightly dividing the word of truth" (2 Tim. 2:15). A careful look at the phrase "approved unto God" indicates a far greater goal perhaps than we have been aware of achieving. To do the best job one is capable of is admirable. To strive to be the kind of teacher God would approve is a challenge that can result in a sincere feeling of inner peace and outward success by the teacher. This challenge also can result in happy, worthwhile learning, and in self-respect on the part of the pupil. Not to just teach "the word of truth," but to teach it right requires genuine study. One must know the needs of each child, what he is like, and how he learns. A good teacher knows teaching methods and available resources.

To Plan

"For want of skillful strategy an army is lost; victory is the fruit of long planning" (Prov. 11:14, NEB). God had a plan as he created the world. He had a plan for Jesus and he has a plan for each of us. God invented planning. He encourages it in his Word. In 1 Corinthians 14:40, we read "Let all things be done decently and in order." Planning is necessary if the pupil is to learn more fully. Someone has said we cannot teach; we can guide learning. Whether we teach (meaning teacher to pupil) or guide learning (meaning teacher and pupil), planning is necessary if there is to be worthwhile results. Planning with fellow teachers is important as we determine common goals for preschoolers.

We plan for everything important to us. We plan for the future of our children as well as ourselves. We plan for Thanksgiving, Christmas, and other holidays. We plan for a vacation and for a dinner party. We even plan for a shopping trip. By our actions, we attest to the fact that we think planning is important. Therefore, planning for such an important assignment as teaching young children is a responsibility not to be taken lightly by preschool teachers. Specific help for planning is available in chapter 4.

To Teach
"Train up a child in the way he should go [and in keeping with his individual gift or bent], and when he is old he will not depart from it" (Prov. 22:6, AMP).[2] We know children are important to God. Again and again children are referred to in the Bible. Jesus demonstrated his love for children as he called them to him and as he rebuked his disciples for sending the children away.

The Scripture quoted above goes a step further than teaching. This translation reminds us that each person is unique and has individual needs and gifts. The teacher will want to discover gifts and interests of each pupil so that he can involve that child in learning. Jesus showed this kind of interest in those he taught. He used examples to which they could relate. The stories and parables of Jesus reflect his awareness of people and their needs. He has been called the Master Teacher. We need look no further for an example. He was and is the supreme example for every teacher.

To Visit
"And he saith unto them, Follow me, and I will make you fishers of men. And they straightway left their nets, and followed him" (Matt. 4:19-20).

For the teacher of preschoolers, the need is to visit to know the child and to get acquainted with parents who, ultimately, make the decision as to whether the child comes to church. Much importance is placed on knowing the child, and this is possible only after seeing the child "on his own turf." Many preschool teachers say they have discovered explanations for the behavior of a child within the first few minutes of a home visit.

Developing a good relationship with parents is valuable. This provides teachers an opportunity to acquaint parents with the church goals and programs for preschoolers. Hopefully, a spirit of cooperation can develop as parents and teachers work together to guide the child, especially in the area of spiritual development.

Visiting in the home can provide teachers with a special challenge to witness to unsaved parents. As one visits, too, ministry opportunities may be discovered that otherwise would not have been shared. Because of these important experiences that await preschool teachers, it is imperative to visit in the home of each preschooler and to cultivate the trust of the parents of preschoolers.

To Witness
"For the Holy Ghost shall teach you in the same hour what ye ought to say" (Luke 12:12).

A CHRISTIAN HOME FOR EVERY PRESCHOOLER

What a goal for all preschool teachers to achieve! How does one go about this task? The answer is uncomplicated and requires only commitment and time. The teacher visits the home of each child assigned to her, and seeks to discover (if not known) the spiritual status of the child's parents. Because of the common bond of the child, teachers often are in the best position of anyone in the church to witness to unsaved parents.

Use of the above Scripture indicates where some preschool teachers hesitate. Preschool teachers have a tendency to think they are not equipped to witness. We may forget to depend on the Holy Spirit to give us the words we are to say. We also need to remember that the best witnessing is done as a Christian shares what Jesus means in his life. Telling someone about his own conversion experience and sharing his joy at being a Christian is the best kind of witnessing a Christian can do. No one else can tell your story like you can. Recall these events before you visit. If you feel more comfortable, mark some Scriptures in your own Bible. The example of your own life and your sincere concern can overshadow any inadequacy you may feel is present in your witnessing. Do not overlook the power of the Holy Spirit. You know you can depend on God. Can he depend on you? One of the greatest gifts a teacher can give to a preschooler is a clear witness for Christ to the child's parents.

To Minister
"Only be sure that you act on the message and do not merely listen; for that would be to mislead yourselves" (Jas. 1:22, NEB).

Ministry opportunities abound. Our job is to make ourselves sensitive and available to them. Visiting in the homes of preschoolers and developing a good relationship with parents is the best way a preschool teacher can make himself available. Demonstrate your availability.
1. Assure parents of your interest and concern.
2. Call or contact a child when he is absent.
3. Always place your name and phone number on literature you leave in the home.
4. Make contact with families during happy times as well as during difficult times.
5. Stay alert to times you can help. Visit regularly.
6. Make specific offers such as baby-sitting when a mother is ill.

Read again the Scripture at the beginning of this chapter (Rom. 12:6-8). Remember that if God has given you the gift of teaching, he has given you the ability to do the job. Remember, too, that God may have called you to teach and now plans for you to prepare yourself through study and experience to fulfill the role. Regardless of your situation, you have been led to read this book with the goal that you can teach preschoolers. Welcome to the most rewarding place of service you can ever have. You may have opportunities:
- To see a baby's eyes light up as you sing the song "God Loves Me"[3]
  - To hear a three-year-old use a Bible thought
    - To listen to a two-year-old sing the song "Jesus Loves Me"[4]
      - To pray with a five-year-old as the two of you look at a book

- To hear a four-year-old say, "Teacher, I love you"
  - To feel the arms of a creeper clasp around your neck
    - To have a toddler run to you from one of his parents
      - To sense the security felt by parents as they place their child in your care

These and many others are the rewards that await the teacher of preschoolers. Responsibilities from God? Indeed they are not. These are privileges that come from Serving God.

Organizing for the Task (Enlistment of Teachers)

A statement read years ago often comes to this writer's mind as enlistment of teachers occurs. The statement was something like this: Give me the right teacher, and everything else will turn out right. Give me the wrong teacher and nothing else matters.

Persons responsible for enlisting preschool teachers want to be constantly looking for the right teachers for preschoolers. Where does one look for the right teachers?

Where Do We Look for Prospective Preschool Teachers?

Adult Sunday School class rolls provide a clue to adults who are faithful in attendance. Adult teachers can provide other helpful information. Persons who teach in Vacation Bible School and are not teaching in Sunday School are good prospects for teaching preschoolers. Observe parents and other adults as they relate to children. Extended sessions provide opportunities for observing adults you may not have other times to observe with children.

Churches with special teacher training groups can provide teachers that are more aware of the responsibilities of teaching and that may be more committed. Become acquainted with the people in this program. Stay in contact with the director so that he can be aware of the need for prepared and dedicated preschool teachers.

Various kinds of survey cards are used by churches to help in discovering people with different kinds of talents and gifts. These cards are most helpful in discovering experienced teachers and those with special talents.

The person responsible for enlisting teachers needs to maintain an ongoing list of potential teachers. As a prospective teacher is encountered, jot down his or her name for future reference.

What Kind of Person Is Desirable as a Teacher of Preschoolers?
Certain characteristics are desirable as we look for potential preschool teachers. Other characteristics are necessary.

Necessary characteristics for the potential preschool teacher include:
 1. Is a Christian and a church member
 2. Likes children
 3. Is dedicated and dependable
 4. Relates well to adults as well as to children
 5. Believes in study and preparation
 6. Is sensitive to the needs of others

Desirable characteristics for the potential preschool teacher include:
 1. Flexibility
 2. Warm and happy personality
 3. Neat appearance
 4. Promptness
 5. Sensibility and confidence
 6. Eagerness to learn

Preschool departments need both men and women as teachers. Each preschool department needs at least one man for some specific reasons:
 1. Men add a sense of security to a room.
 2. Some preschoolers respond more quickly to men.
 3. Preschoolers need to hear and see men teaching the Bible.
 4. Many preschoolers live in homes without a father and need a man to whom they can relate.
 5. Some preschoolers need a good example set by a man.
 6. Men can develop a good relationship with unsaved parents and especially the young fathers.

Ladies, the above paragraph is not meant to minimize the important role you play in preschool departments. You make up the greater percentage of teachers and have the God-given gift of warmth and "mothering" that are absolutely necessary with young children. Your sensitivity enables you to know when a child needs a hug, a smile, or an encouraging word. You can understand better the plight of a young mother who stays home all week with a new baby or with three preschoolers. You can lend to mothers of preschoolers a listening ear, and sometimes, a helping hand.

Enlisting Directors and Teachers

Southern Baptist Churches have various ways of enlisting potential teachers. Most churches work through nominating committees. You will want to comply with the appropriate method used in your church as you have vacancies occur in the department in which you serve. Read chapter 4 of the book *Basic Preschool Work* by Jerry Terrell for detailed help in discovery and enlistment of directors and teachers.

Responsibilities of Directors

Regardless of who enlists directors and teachers, responsibilities of the position need to be shared at the time of enlistment. If you are the director of a department, you need to know that your responsibilities include:
- Planning, conducting, and evaluating the work of the department.
- Cooperating with the nominating committee in enlisting and training teachers.
- Leading weekly workers' meetings and organizing for effective teaching, outreach, and ministry.
- Maintaining department records, assigning to the teachers names of preschoolers and their families to be visited.
- Directing Sunday sessions including group time in the departments for threes, fours, and fives.
- Organizing for the distribution of periodicals appropriate for the age of the preschooler and for parents.
- Requesting and administering appropriate funds for the department.
- Enlisting extended session teachers and guiding in planning for effective teaching if the department has these sessions.
- Planning training events to help teachers improve their skills.
- Representing the department at the meeting for outreach leaders as well as at special church council and committee meetings.

Responsibilities of Teachers

Teachers will want to know their responsibilities include:
- Attending the weekly workers' meetings, assisting the de-

partment director in carrying out the work of the department.
- Teaching during the session, assisting as needed during group time in departments for threes, fours, and fives.
- Participating in room preparation and the gathering of materials for each session.
- Visiting and ministering to assigned preschoolers and their families.
- Assisting in reaching prospects for the department and sharing prospect information with appropriate age groups to help them reach other family members.
- Notifying the department director as early as possible when you must be absent.
- Obtaining a substitute teacher when your absence is necessary.
- Taking turns with others in the department in leading during the extended session if the department has one.

Other Leadership Positions

Several other positions of leadership may be needed in a Preschool Division. The need varies with the size of the division and the size of the church. You may have been asked to be the Preschool Division director or outreach leader. Perhaps you have been asked to be the Cradle Roll department director or a visitor-teacher. Specific responsibilities are spelled out for these important tasks in chapter 4 of the book *Basic Preschool Work.*

Remember that regardless of what you have been asked to do in a preschool department, you are a teacher. Preschoolers will be learning from you. Some adults have overlooked the simple truth that preschoolers are in a constant learning process. They learn from everyone with whom they come in contact. It is important for those of us who teach them in church programs to keep this thought in mind.

A Look at Why Preschool Teachers Come and Go

"I need to talk with you," Nancy said as we passed in the hall after the Sunday morning session. "I will call you tomorrow," I responded, feeling I knew what the conversation would include. I thought about this young teacher who had taught in a preschool department for the last six months. She had started teaching after our last study course, therefore there had been no planned training session from which she could learn. Her department director had had family problems and had not been having regularly scheduled workers' meetings. When there had been planning meetings, so much needed to be discussed that no time was left for training or evaluation. Teachers in the department had not been led or encouraged to be involved in outreach.

My conversation with Nancy was no surprise. She had decided to go back to her Sunday School class. She did not feel she was doing much in the way of teaching. She needed the companionship of others her own age, and she missed the Bible study. These were her reasons. I thought of the many preschool directors and teachers who served year after year. I thought of preschool leaders in many churches who talk about the difficulty of enlisting and keeping teachers. There has to be a solution. Perhaps these thoughts can help both directors and teachers.

The list could go on and on. Hopefully, the answer is evident. Teachers become discouraged when they do not understand what they are doing. An untrained teacher cannot always understand what is being accomplished even when good teaching is being done in the department. Christians are called to reach as well as to teach and can have a sense of being successful through involvement in ministry and outreach.

Department director, your role in leading the teachers in your department in a weekly workers' meeting and in visiting, witnessing, and ministering is a very important one. Of equal importance is the need to see that training opportunities are provided.

Teacher, your role includes committing yourself to attend the weekly workers' meetings and to do your share of the visiting, witnessing, and ministering. In reality, teacher, you are responsible for developing the gifts and skills God has given you. Your church can plan training sessions, but you must make the decision to attend. Your denomination can produce the study books and lesson materials but you make the decision to read and to study them.

Why, then, do preschool teachers come and go? Perhaps it is because some become discouraged from not being able to see what they are accomplishing. Until preschool teachers study and understand the preschool child, they may have difficulty seeing worthwhile results of their teaching. Maybe some need to have more expected of them. Every teacher needs to know in advance the responsibilities of the position.

As a teacher called to teach preschoolers, you are sensitive and concerned about your responsibility. You expect to see results

THOUGHT	REMEDY
1. Methods of teaching preschoolers are structured in accordance with the way the child learns and may be different from what some adults are accustomed to in the classroom.	1. A study of the books *Understanding Today's Preschoolers* and *How to Guide Preschoolers* can help teachers understand the importance of their job.
2. Ongoing spiritual growth and Bible study is necessary for every Christian.	2. Special times for Bible study planned and encouraged. A time for Bible background study during weekly workers' meeting.
3. Fellowship with other Christians is needed, especially in the mobile society in which we live.	3. Fellowship should be encouraged among preschooler teachers. Adult departments need to be reminded to keep in touch with the adults in service who would be in the department age range.
4. A dedicated, serious teacher wants to see results.	4. Evaluation during weekly planning meetings can help a new or inexperienced teacher realize what to look for in the results of her teaching.
5. A called teacher needs to be involved in outreach and ministry.	5. The department director must lead others in the department to visit and to minister.
6. People of today are accustomed to goal setting and achievement.	6. Our goals in teaching preschoolers need to be shared. Specific teaching aims in the lesson material need to be emphasized.

and to feel successful. These can come as you become acquainted with parents and with your teaching goals. A Preschool Division director visited in the home of a two-and one-half-year-old. She was pleased as the parents told her statements about the Bible and church made by their child. These parents were especially pleased about the child's wanting his turn during prayer times. The parents were amazed that this much learning was taking place. The division director thought of the people this child encounters at church: teachers on Sunday morning and evening, special helpers to provide guidance and care during the week, extended session teachers, and other adults. These are the people in the most important business of a lifetime—the business of laying a basic spiritual foundation in a young life. Because you are the *right teacher,* the opportunities will be yours.

---

[1] From *The New English Bible.* Copyright © The Delegates of the Oxford University Press and the Syndics of the Cambridge University Press, 1961, 1970. Reprinted by permission. Subsequent quotations are marked NEB.
[2] From *The Amplified Bible,* Old Testament. Copyright © 1962, 1964 by Zondervan Publishing House. Used by permission.
[3] Tune "God Loves Me," *More Songs for 4's & 5's.* p. 6.
[4] Tune "Jesus Loves Me," *More Songs for 4's & 5's.* p. 41.

Chapter 3
The Door to Teaching Preschoolers the Bible

The worship service continued as the music leader asked the congregation to stand and join in singing a familiar hymn. As we sang the song, my attention was caught by a five-year-old standing two pews in front of where I was standing. I could tell by watching the movement of his mouth that he was singing every word, especially the chorus. I thought about how this child had learned this song he was singing. He had, no doubt, heard it sung many times, having been in the worship service with his parents since the age of three- and one-half. He knew the chorus and sang it with more confidence, meaning he had learned first the more often repeated words. I thought about other things he had learned as he had observed his parents in prayer and in praise. He had learned from the examples set by his parents and others who were worshiping. Obviously he had learned that he was a part of this service just as others were a part. He had heard many words with which he was familiar. True, he may not have understood everything that was happening, but he was sensing attitudes and feelings that would affect his decisions and choices for the rest of his life.

The Preschooler and Learning

We know that learning is the acquisition of knowledge, information, or skill, and that learning produces change. In my copy of the book *Understanding Today's Preschoolers* by C. Sybil Waldrop, I have underlined several outstanding statements from page 74 on this subject:

"The more one learns, the more he is able to learn."

"The mind has an incredible and largely untapped capacity for learning."

"The mind is developed largely through information taken in from the senses and the body's movement."

"The first five years are crucial to development of the mind."

"Telling as a means of teaching is empty unless the child is given the opportunity to learn by doing."[1]

Guiding the preschooler to learn requires a knowledge of what he is like at each age level, what his needs are, and how he learns. These subjects are explored completely in *Understanding Today's Preschoolers*, a must for you to read. However, because of their effect on the learning of the preschoolers, they merit our review. Perhaps the following chart can be helpful.

Basic Needs of Preschoolers	General Characteristics of Preschoolers	Ways Preschoolers Learn
Love	Active	Relationships with others
Guidance and Control	Creative	Senses
Acceptance	Imitative	Imitating
Security	Curious	Curiosity
Sense of Trust	Imaginaive	Repetition
Self-Respect	Sensitive	Doing
Dependence	Short Attention Span	Playing
Independence	Literal-Minded	Satisfaction

Obviously, then, if the child is to learn, these known facts will determine the teaching method.

Learning Through Relationships with Others

The child is learning from adults and from his peers. He learns from the examples set by teachers and parents. The child learns as he interacts with other boys and girls.

Example 1: A teacher sings as she changes the diapers of a three-monh-old. Mark hears his name as the teacher sings, "Jesus, Jesus, I love Jesus. Jesus, Jesus, he loves Mark."[2] Mark begins to feel better physically. He likes his teacher's smile and the song. He recognizes his name and hears it along with other words such as love and Jesus. Mark is learning that he is loved and that people at church are friends he can trust. He is learning that at church he is happy, safe, comfortable.

Example 2: John and Mike are building with blocks in the four-year department. Each has his own structure. Nathan joins the group and pulls from the shelf the remaining blocks. "I need some more blocks," says Mike to the teacher nearby. "What can we do to help Mike?" the teacher asks as she looks at John. "I'll give him some of my blocks," responds John, handing several blocks to Mike. Nathan follows John's example. Soon the three boys become involved in one project. These boys have learned to respect the rights of others. They have learned that working together and sharing produces happy results.

Learning Through the Senses
All that preschoolers learn is through one or more of the five senses. Because of this, it is important to provide many sensory experiences. Listening to music, reading a book, tasting an unfamiliar food, watching a goldfish, smelling a flower, and feeling a furry animal are the kinds of firsthand experiences needed if learning is to take place in a preschool room.

Example 1: A five-year-old discovers several red apples on the nature shelf. "What are we going to do with these?" she asks. The teacher says, "What would you like to do?" "Let's eat them," comes the eager response. As others show interest, the children are guided to wash the apples. Two plastic knives are used as the boys and girls take turns cutting the apples. The teacher guides the conversation to include observing the seed inside and God's plan for us to plant seed so that trees can grow. He encourages the children to smell the apples and to talk about the red color. The group is led to express their thanks to God before tasting the apples. Obvious learning has taken place.

Example 2: The teacher of toddlers brings to her room a box of fall leaves. The toddlers enjoy putting both hands in the leaves. They realize the leaves can be crushed and enjoy this activity. As the toddlers play, the teacher sings, "See the leaves falling, They fall all around; See the leaves falling, They fall to the ground."[3] "Thank you, God, for pretty leaves," the teacher says. These toddlers have learned by feeling the leaves. They have heard the words that tell about the leaves and they have enjoyed this experience at church. Their thoughtful teacher has helped them associate God with happy feelings.

Learning by Imitating
Children love to imitate—to play like. They imitate important people in their lives. They imitate teachers, parents, older children, and other special people. The homeliving materials and area in a preschool room provide opportunities for playing out

and for imitating others.

Example: Four-year-old Benjamin discovers a mail bag with letters in it in the homeliving area. On a nearby wall is a picture of a letter carrier. Benjamin places a bag (a woman's shoulder bag) on his shoulder and delivers the mail. He is learning about special helpers in his world. He is learning about ways God provides for him and for his family.

Learning Through Curiosity

The child gets into a lot of trouble because of his natural curiosity. Adults may misunderstand his natural curiosity and miss opportunities to guide him in learning experiences. He wants to know how the clock ticks, what the electrical outlet does, and what can happen if he pulls on the lamp cord. Young preschoolers explore by tasting, whether it is the lamp cord or the dog's ear. Teachers can take advantage of this special gift of curiosity by providing safe materials to stimulate questions and to motivate involvement in learning. The child whose curiosity can be stimulated to cause him to ask questions may be more ready to listen or to explore answers. Curiosity is the beginning of discovery. The wise teacher places materials in the room, then allows the children to discover them. In this way, it becomes their idea or question. One of the challenging aspects of teaching preschoolers is the opportunity to provide materials that can stimulate the child's natural curiosity. When successful, this experience results in worthwhile learning.

Example: One Sunday a tadpole in a small fishbowl was placed on the nature shelf. The children enjoyed watching the tadpole swim about, but were not really interested in what he might become. On the following Sunday, the teacher noted that the tadpole now had two very obvious legs. She said nothing. It did not take five-year-old Tim long to discover the legs and to let everyone in the room know about his discovery. Several children gathered around the nature shelf asking questions and sharing in the experience. The teacher had a group of eager learners participating in a discussion about God's plan for tadpoles to grow. The natural opportunity to refer to a Bible thought and to use other Bible-related conversation was the result.

Learning by Repetition

The child learns a new skill by repetition or practice. He does not learn to drink from a cup or to tie his shoe the first time he

tries. He devlops a new skill, then refines that skill by repeating it again and again. Words to songs and Bible stories are also learned by repetition.
Example: Four-year-old Don was having a hard time working the puzzle he had chosen. The teacher encouraged him with suggestions about looking for certain pieces and turning the pieces in different directions until he had completed his puzzle. "Don, you did a good job working that hard puzzle," was the teacher's commendation as Don finished the puzzle. Much to the teacher's surprise, Don immediately took the pieces out again and started to work the puzzle. After working the same puzzle several times, Don then proceeded to work the wooden inlay puzzle outside the tray. He was refining his skills and enjoying his latest step in building self-esteem. The teacher found a natural opportunity to say, "Thank you, God, for helping Don learn to work hard puzzles."

Because they learn by repetition, preschoolers need to be told simple guidelines again and again. This also helps them feel more secure as they hear the same guidelines repeated from week to week.

Learning by Doing
Learning by doing means having a firsthand experience. It means tasting apples, feeling fall leaves, and watching a tadpole become a frog. Books and pictures on each of these subjects are available. Yet, the young child is not ready to take a picture and mentally relate it to the real object until he has experienced the real thing.
Example: The Church Training leader had placed in the home-living area the necessary materials for making applesauce. Several boys and girls joined in the fun of making applesauce. Many learning experiences resulted. A comment by one child is the part of this story that is significant. It was decided that the applesauce needed to cool and should be shared by everyone during group time. As the children ate the applesauce, one child said, "I didn't know applesauce came from apples."

Learning Through Play
Play is the work of the child. Children work harder at playing than anything they do. This learning through play provides adults with a special entrance to teaching. As the child plays with the various kinds of teaching materials the teacher provides, he

can put into practice those Bible thoughts shared with him by his teachers. What is important at this age is that the child is learning how to apply Bible truths and thoughts he is hearing to experiences in his room at church and in his everyday life. Some preschoolers may be capable of memorization. Memorizing Scripture at this age may result in adult approval. Applying Bible truths to everyday life will result in God's approval, and in happiness for self and others. Look for opportunities to apply Bible truths.

This story was shared with a group of preschool teachers by Miss Nora Padgett. A teacher of fours and fives, it seems, had a tendency to use one Bible thought much more than she used others. This thought, from 1 Timothy 6:18, was "Be ready to share." During the session the teacher used the thought several times. One child was overheard saying to another, "You don't have to talk about it so much. You just give somebody some of what you've got." Perhaps adults can benefit from less talking and more doing!

Learning Through Satisfaction
As the child experiences success, he is encouraged to move on to greater things. It is important that materials in a preschool department be on the developmental level of the age group in the room. Children need to be commended when they accomplish a task. They need teachers who encourage them to try again when they are unsuccessful the first time. Don's working the puzzle is a good example of the result of a feeling of satisfaction.

Preschoolers can be taught the Bible through the same ways they learn other things. Bible verses, thoughts, and conversation can be applied as the child is involved in everyday situations. A child of two or three can be taught to quote a Bible verse such as Ephesians 4:32. However, learning has not taken place until the child can apply the concept of *being kind* to people in his everyday life. Anyone who wishes can quote the Bible. Understanding it and putting it into practice in life is our goal for preschoolers.

Teaching Through Activities
Teaching is done through the various kinds of educationally sound materials placed in a room for preschoolers. As preschoolers use these materials and interact with one another, teachers apply Bible thoughts, songs, and conversation to enrich the learning that is taking place. Providing a choice of activities

follows a developmental principle in that no two children are alike. Therefore, what one child chooses to do may not be what the next one will choose. When allowed to choose an activity they enjoy, the learning experience will be a happier one for most preschoolers. Another conclusion is that preschoolers should not be expected to do the same thing at the same time, such as all of them making the same picture. The exception is that three-, four-, and five-year-olds participate in a large group activity. Methods used and materials provided for a specific age group are used because of the level of readiness at that age.

Activity areas suggested for use with twos, threes, fours, and fives are music, nature, books, homeliving, puzzles, blocks, and art. Suggestions of appropriate materials to help accomplish specific Bible teaching aims can be found in *Preschool Bible Teacher A*, *Preschool Bible Teacher B*, *Preschool Bible Teacher C*, and *Bible Story Time at Church*. In the book, *How to Guide Preschoolers*, a separate chapter is devoted to discussing each of these activities. Values gained from participating in the activity are explored and ways to use the materials are suggested. Teachers may want to make the study of this book a priority.

Enriching the Activity Experience

As preschoolers discover and explore the materials provided by their teachers, they usually become involved in the activity in one way or another: a creeper or toddler may examine the stacking cone with both his hands and with his mouth. A three-year-old may choose to put on the adult dress and shoes she finds in the homeliving area. A five-year-old may locate a smock and join in the painting activity in the art area. Regardless of which activity the preschooler chooses or what direction the play takes, a teacher will want to be nearby to offer guidelines in the use of the materials and to apply Bible truths.

Appropriately interweaving Bible teaching into the child's play or activity is perhaps the greatest challenge of all to a preschool teacher. Ways of being prepared to enrich the child's experiences are suggested in chapter 4 of this book.

Several terms are used to identify the approach of interweaving into children's play biblically based content. Some of these terms are "guidance suggestions," "interwoven activities," and "teachable moments." Teachers may set the stage for many of these opportunities. Teachers will want to be ready to recognize these when they occur naturally, creating teachable moments.

Methods to enrich learning through interwoven activities are:
- Repeating Bible stories, thoughts, and verses.
- Utilizing conversation.
- Showing pictures.
- Singing songs.
- Using prayer.
- Utilizing guidance and instruction.

The teacher may use these methods from the moment a preschooler enters the room until he departs. Singing "I Am Happy"[4] helps a child feel good about himself as he arrives in his room. The Bible thought "God made us" (Ps. 100:3) may be shared as the toddler or creeper examines the stacking cone. As the three-year-old dresses herself in the adult dress and shoes, the teacher may say, "Those are clothes like mothers wear. Thank you, God, for mothers." As the five-year-old uses the art materials, a teacher may say, "I like the colors you are using. God is good to us to help us have many pretty colors."

Opportunities for teaching preschoolers the Bible are endless. The wise teacher desires to be as prepared as possible by providing appropriate materials and by planning ways to accomplish the Bible teaching aims for each month.

Teaching the Bible Through Large-Group Experiences
Ways of teaching preschoolers Bible truths during group time are more easily identified than during activity time. Both are of equal importance. Large group experiences are suggested for three-, four-, and five-year-olds. Group time is suggested as the last part of a session for preschoolers. It is the responsibility of the department director and is usually led by that person. Elements of the Group Time:
- Bible stories and Bible conversation
- Bible thoughts and verses
- Music and songs
- Conversation
- Pictures
- Games and relaxation activities
- Child experience stories
- Prayer
- Filmstrips

The age group teaching guides make adequate suggestions for ways to use the Bible as the above elements are used during large group experiences with preschoolers. Chapter 13 in the book

How to Guide Preschoolers is written to assist the teacher responsible in directing group time. All teachers in a preschool department will want to read this chapter.

Teachers in the department have important responsibilities for group time. Teachers encourage preschoolers to put away materials and to join the large group, making the transition between activity time and group time as smooth as possible. Teachers should sit in the semicircle with the children during group time, unless there is a space problem. Teachers can support the director by listening and by participating in the activities of group time. A teacher in the semicircle is the one to remind the child who is not listening or to encourage another to participate, leaving the director free to lead the entire group.

The Learning Environment
The room he comes to at church has an important effect on the child's learning. His room is "the church" to the young preschooler. Whether the church has one room or twenty rooms for preschoolers, a good environment can be provided. As a teacher, you are responsible for making the place assigned to preschoolers you teach as attractive and ready to teach in as possible. Study chapters 12, 13, 14, 15, 16, and 17 of *Basic Preschool Work* to help you meet the challenge of providing the best possible space and environment for learning. The following suggestions are to help you evaluate your own situation:
1. The room is well lighted and ventilated.
2. Windows are low enough for the child to see out, when possible.
3. Floors need to be clean and rooms clear of clutter.
4. Maintain constant safety precautions: be alert to broken toys, open doors, exposed electrical outlets, cleaning materials, and other kinds of dangers to preschoolers.
5. Pictures are to be on the child's eye level or on the floor. Pictures placed high on walls may lose some of their effectiveness.
6. Preschoolers need space to move: thirty-five square feet recommended for each person enrolled. Even in a church with limited space, a minimum of twenty square feet is needed.
7. Teaching materials need to provide challenge and opportunities to be successful.
8. The room is ready when the first child arrives.

9. The room conveys a message; "Come in to your room, we are ready and waiting for YOU."
10. Furnishings and equipment are proportioned to the age and developmental stage of children in the room.

You may be the person in your church responsible for preschool ministry. You may be the director of a preschool department in a one-room church. Whatever your place of service, obtain a copy of *Basic Preschool Work* to find more details on the recommended space, room arrangements, and suggested lists of materials and supplies to help you and your church provide for preschoolers.

Teacher Resources

Resources to help you be a better teacher are plentiful and provide opportunities for teachers to study together or to teach themselves. Southern Baptists have a unique educational system whereby a person can follow a course of study and become skilled in teaching a specific age group. This plan is called the Church Study Course. The *Church Study Course Catalog* is a free booklet available from your state Sunday School department office. All courses and required books are listed in this catalog that suggests many kinds of courses of study.

Books to help teachers of preschoolers include *Basic Preschool Work* by Jerry Terrell. This book can help teachers in organization, administration, and in providing a good learning environment. This book, as well as all those written to help teachers of preschoolers, can help in understanding the child and our goals for teaching. Harry Piland says, "Reaching, teaching, and ministry are the heartbeat of the book."[5]

How to Guide Preschoolers, compiled by Jenell Strickland, was written by several capable, experienced preschool teachers and leaders. Cos Davis says, "The book is a successful attempt to help teachers of preschoolers understand the reasons for and the methods of communicating biblical truths to preschoolers through activities."[6]

Understanding Today's Preschoolers, by C. Sybil Waldrop, is a must for both teachers and parents of preschoolers. It focuses on the growth and development of preschoolers, the importance of family and others, the processes of learning, principles of guiding preschoolers, and ways to minister to preschoolers with special needs. This book answers questions you may have been (or will be) asked such as:

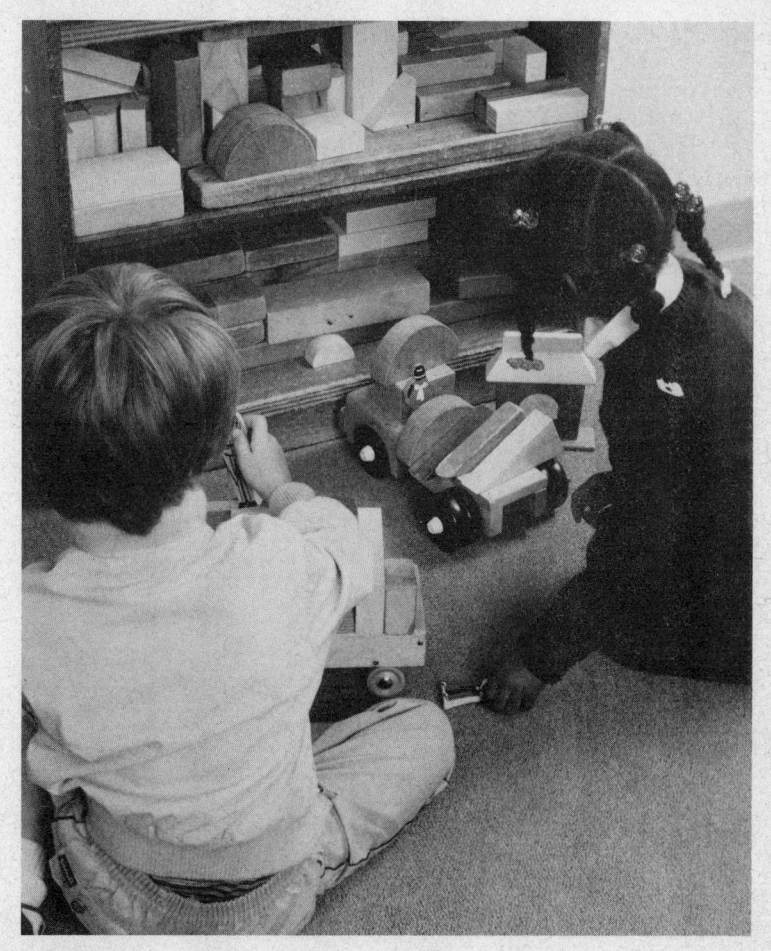

"How can preschoolers learn Bible truths when all they do is play?"

"What can an infant learn at church?"

"Why are not preschoolers encouraged to memorize Scripture?"

A special book for Cradle Roll workers is *Cradle Roll = Visitation* by Jewell Wells Nelson. This book covers the organization and working of a Cradle Roll. The book has many good ideas and suggestions for all preschool teachers.

Reaching Preschoolers, Jenell Strickland, compiler, places the proper importance on reaching preschoolers and their families. This book provides a biblical basis for reaching and offers practical help on how to get the job done.

New books in the study course series are planned periodically.

The process of producing new books is one way The Sunday School Board of the Southern Baptist Convention helps teachers keep up-to-date and prepared to teach. A comparison of any of these age-group books, whether on child development or methods of teaching, with secular books on the same subject, can help you be assured that Southern Baptists are educationally sound and current in the methods and philosophies of preschool education. We can trust the materials provided by our Convention to help us do the job God has called us to do.

In addition to the books mentioned here, hundreds of others are available to help teachers in personal growth and in other ways to become better teachers. Directors or others responsible for training teachers, or those enlisted to teach one of these books, can find additional help in resource kits accompanying selected study course books.

A set of four filmstrips is available to help teachers be more efficient in their work with preschoolers. Titled "How to Teach Preschoolers in Sunday School Series," the filmstrips are *Teaching Preschoolers Through Activities; Understanding the Preschool Child; You, A Teacher of Preschoolers;* and *Planning for Effective Teaching of Preschoolers. Using Bible Story Time Curriculum* can help those preschool teachers using Bible Story Time materials. A filmstrip to help preschool teachers in witnessing by the title of *Winning Parents of Preschoolers* is also available.

Other filmstrips that can help preschool teachers are:
Extended Session for Preschoolers
Reach Out to Preschoolers
Reach Out with Cradle Roll
Teaching Babies and Toddlers
Teaching Twos and Threes
Teaching Fours and Fives

Be alert to other new filmstrips being produced to help preschool teachers grow and develop.

Tools for Teaching
The Bible is the guidebook for the preschool teacher. A wealth of additional material awaits teachers for use in helping preschoolers understand and apply the Bible to their lives. Some-

times called curriculum, sometimes called literature, this material is published quarterly by The Baptist Sunday School Board. There are two curriculum series for preschool teachers to choose. The use and purpose of this material is fully discussed in chapters 10 and 11 in the book *Basic Preschool Work*. A chart of materials available for each age group can help new teachers become aware of the materials available to assist them in their responsibility.

Preschool Leadership is a magazine published quarterly to aid preschool staff persons and directors in administering preschool programs. The July-August-September issue provides an overview of the Sunday School and Church Training preschool curriculum for the next year.

BTN is a means by which The Sunday School Board can communicate directly with churches and associations by satellite. Inspirational, educational, and informational messages are sent to participating churches.

Bible Story Time curriculum materials are available for churches that may have one or more of the following arrangements: Combined age groups, limited space, limited resources. For example, a church with one or two preschool departments for the birth through five-year age span can benefit from considering this line of literature since specific help is given for a wider age span.

One of the eight scope areas is used as the subject for each Bible-centered unit of study in curriculum for preschoolers. This area is usually identifiable in the title. Bible teaching objectives are stated at the beginning of each unit of study. This determines for the teacher a specific goal for the month. To accomplish these goals, methods and materials are suggested in each teaching guide. These suggestions are based on biblical accuracy, sound educational principles, and the age and needs of the learner.

---

[1] C. Sybil Waldrop, *Understanding Today's Preschoolers.* (Nashville: Convention Press, 1982), p. 74.
[2] Tune "Jesus, Jesus," *Songs for the Young Child.* p. 16.
[3] Words by Alma May Scarborough. Music by Nettie Lou Jones. © Copyright 1961, The Sunday School Board of the Southern Baptist Convention. All rights reserved. Used by permission.
[4] Tune "I Am Happy," *Songs for the Young Child.* p. 38.
[5] Jerry Terrell, *Basic Preschool Work.* (Nashville: Convention Press, 1981), p. 2.
[6] Jenell Strickland, comp., *How to Guide Preschoolers.* (Nashville: Convention Press, 1982), p. 4.

Age Group	Literature Piece	Purpose or Intended User
Babies, Creepers, Toddlers	*Preschool Bible Teacher A*	A teaching guide for teachers of this age group
	Preschool Bible Teacher A Resource Kit	Contains teaching aids for teachers' use
	Preschool Pictures A, Set 1	20 pictures to be used with preschoolers
	Preschool Pictures A, Set 2	20 pictures to be used with preschoolers
	Preschool Pictures A, Set 3	20 pictures to be used with preschoolers
	Beginning	Home book for parents to use with babies, creepers, and toddlers
	Extended Session for Babies, and Toddlers	For those teaching during the extended session
Twos and Threes	*Preschool Bible Teacher B*	A teaching guide for teachers of this age group
	Preschool Bible Teacher B Resource Kit	Contains teaching aids for teachers' use
	Preschool Pictures B, Set 1	30 pictures to be used with twos and threes
	Preschool Pictures B, Set 2	20 pictures to be used with twos and threes
	Living	A home book for parents to use with twos and threes
	Extended Session for 2's and 3's	For those teaching during the extended session
Fours and Fives	*Preschool Bible Teacher C*	A teaching guide for teachers of this age group
	Preschool Bible Teacher C Resource Kit	Contains teaching aids for teachers' use

Age Group	Literature Piece	Purpose or Intended User
Fours and Fives	*Preschool Pictures C, Set 1* *Preschool Pictures C, Set 2* *Preschool Pictures C, Set 3* *Preschool Pictures C, Set 4* *Growing* *Look and Listen* *Extended Session for 4's and 5's*	20 pictures to be used with older preschoolers 20 pictures to be used with older preschoolers 20 pictures to be used with older preschoolers 20 pictures to be used with older preschoolers Home book for parents to use with 4's and 5's Pull apart enrichment leaflets with multiple uses For those teaching during extended session
Cradle Roll	*Messages for Parents-to-Be* *Cradle Roll Poster Set* *Cradle Roll Poster Set, No. 2* *Beginning* *Home Life*	6 booklets to be delivered to the home 6 posters to help promote Cradle Roll awareness 6 posters focusing on special days of the year A quarterly magazine to take into the homes of Cradle Roll members A monthly magazine that can be taken to the home
All Programs	*Preschool Leadership* *Living with Preschoolers*	A quarterly magazine containing helpful information for preschool directors, volunteer coordinators, and preschool staff persons (Sunday School and Church Training) A magazine to be delivered to the homes of preschoolers containing articles for parents

Age Group	Literature Piece	Purpose or Intended User
Babies through Fives	*Bible Story Time at Church* *Bible Story Time at Church Resource Kit* *Refer to "All Programs" List in preceding chart for other materials.	A teaching guide for teachers of birth through two-year-olds, three-year-olds through five-year-olds, or birth through five-year-olds Prepared resources for teachers of babies through five-year-olds (Kit items may be shared between two departments.)
Babies through Twos	*Bible Stories for Me*	Pupils' leaflets containing Bible stories, thoughts, and Bible-related activities
Threes through Fives	*Bible Story Time at Home*	Pupils' leaflets containing Bible stories, thoughts, and Bible-related activities

Chapter 4
Planning to Teach Preschoolers the Bible

"Plans fail for lack of counsel, but with many advisers they succeed" (Prov. 15:22, NIV).[1]

"Plan carefully what you do and whatever you do will turn out right" (Prov. 4:26, GNB).[2]

"Commit to the Lord whatever you do, and your plans will succeed" (Prov. 16:3, NIV).

Planning is important whether one is taking a trip across the United States or baking a cake. Who among us would start out on a trip with his family to drive across our country and make no plans in advance? Who among us would begin the simple process of baking a cake from a recipe not used before without reading the directions and checking for necessary tools and ingredients? Who among us would want to approach another Sunday of opportunities to teach preschoolers from the Bible without having made careful plans?

It has been suggested that the peak learning age of the child is two years and seven months. Of course, at this time the child is learning to speak a language, to feed himself, and many other skills that remain throughout his lifetime. How much of the child's readiness to learn can teachers at church take advantage of at this age? What is more important for a preschooler to learn than that he is special and is loved by God and that at church he feels important? Preparation to teach preschoolers is crucial when one remembers that what is put into the first of life remains and affects the rest of life. In the filmstrip *Reach Out to Preschoolers,* Willa Ruth Garlow says, "Poor teaching sends more people out the back door of our churches than a good outreach can bring in the front door."[3] In the filmstrip *Planning for Effective Teaching of Preschoolers,* Sue Raley notes, "Good planning does not ensure results, but it makes them far more possible."[4] As teachers, called by God, we want to do all we can to ensure good results from our teaching. Preparation is an important ingredient of success.

Regular Planning
The weekly workers' meeting is the most successful method available to provide adequate planning for teaching, reaching, and ministering to preschoolers and their families. Positive results of an effective planning meeting are listed below.
- Successful teaching
- Witnessing-Ministering opportunities shared
- Training together means consistency for preschoolers
- Evaluation of the work of the department
- Development of a team spirit
- Fellowship with other adults
- Communication between teachers, parents, and children
- Coordination of the department goals and tasks

Good tools are available to help you plan. Chapter 6 in *Basic Preschool Work* answers the who, what, when, and where questions of planning. The filmstrip *Planning for Effective Teaching of Preschoolers* provides an overall view of department planning and points out results that can be expected from an effective meeting. *Preschool Bible Teacher A, Preschool Bible Teacher B, Preschool Bible Teacher C* and *Bible Story Time at Church* provide regular planning suggestions for the director to use in leading these sessions. *Preschool Leadership* includes weekly suggestions for division and department directors for regular planning meetings.

The department director is the person responsible for leading the department planning meeting. The director may find these suggestions (see chart) helpful:

Suggestions for an Effective Workers' Meeting	
Suggestion	**Example**
1. Generate a positive attitude.	"Jim, you're going to like teaching in our department. Our weekly planning meeting is one of our strongest points."
2. Establish expectations.	"The Bible teaching aim for this month is exciting. I will see you at workers' meeting Wednesday night so that we can plan to use some of the good suggestions."
3. Make meetings worthwhile.	Begin and end the meeting on time. Plan the agenda. Allot time for each segment.
4. Let teachers participate.	Ask a teacher to review Bible background on one of the stories. Ask a teacher to demonstrate one of the art activities. Assign teachers to bring suggested materials to the meeting.

Suggestions for an Effective Workers' Meeting	
Suggestion	Example
5. Make use of variety.	Place a sign at the door to the department. The sign may say "STOP, get on your knees, evaluate our room from the eye level of preschoolers." Avoid using the same procedure for every planning meeting.
6. Provide resources.	Provide plan sheets for teachers to complete. Locate the suggested books and/or recordings.
7. Encourage fellowship.	Allow time for some fellowship at the beginning or end of a meeting. Lead in planning for a fellowship at another time, thus encouraging taking advantage of planning time as well as teaching time on Sunday.
8. Encourage communication.	Listen to what is being said (even if it means reading between the lines). Develop a relationship that encourages Christian openness and cooperation.

Just as it is important to have a weekly workers' meeting, it is also important to plan the meeting well. We live in a busy, complex world. Most people attend the same kinds of meetings more than once if they continue to benefit from the meetings. Director, you can find specific help for planning the meeting in the teaching guide for the age group with which you work.

Elements of a Good Planning Meeting
Knowing the elements of a good planning meeting can help the person leading in the planning to properly allot time segments

for each element. Because of the different needs within each church, there is no suggested time or order for these elements. However, a suggested order may be found in the teaching guide. *Preschool Leadership* offers help in planning weekly workers' meetings. Each of the following elements should be a part of each suggested meeting:

- *Inspiration* may involve a review of the Bible background for the story on Sunday, singing a suggested song, or a prayer time.
- *Reaching, witnessing, ministering* reports and assignments can be discussed and shared. Visitors and prospects may be assigned. Ministry opportunities can be determined and planned. Brainstorm ways of reaching families. Review tracts which may be helpful in witnessing.
- *Administration* includes sharing information about the total church program. Preschool teachers need to be involved in other programs of the church. They need to be kept up-to-date on church, associational, and state level happenings among Southern Baptists. Administration of division and department concerns may be noted.
- *Planning for teaching and learning* includes gathering materials, locating pictures, preparing the room, and other actions necessary to being ready for the coming session. Plan for training segments during a portion of this time. Evaluate the last session.

The weekly workers' meeting is for preschool teachers who have as their goal to do the best job possible in teaching preschoolers. Teachers have specific responsibilities toward this meeting just as directors have. This meeting is planned for teachers with the ultimate goal being Bible-centered learning on the part of the child. What can teachers do to enhance the effectiveness of the weekly workers' meeting?

- The teacher can *pray* for God's leadership in planning and in teaching.
- The teacher can *study* ahead the curriculum materials so that he may be ready for the meeting.
- The teacher can put forth every effort to *attend* all weekly workers' meetings.
- The teacher can *participate* in the meeting.
- The teacher can *evaluate* himself and the work of the department so that success in teaching preschoolers will result.

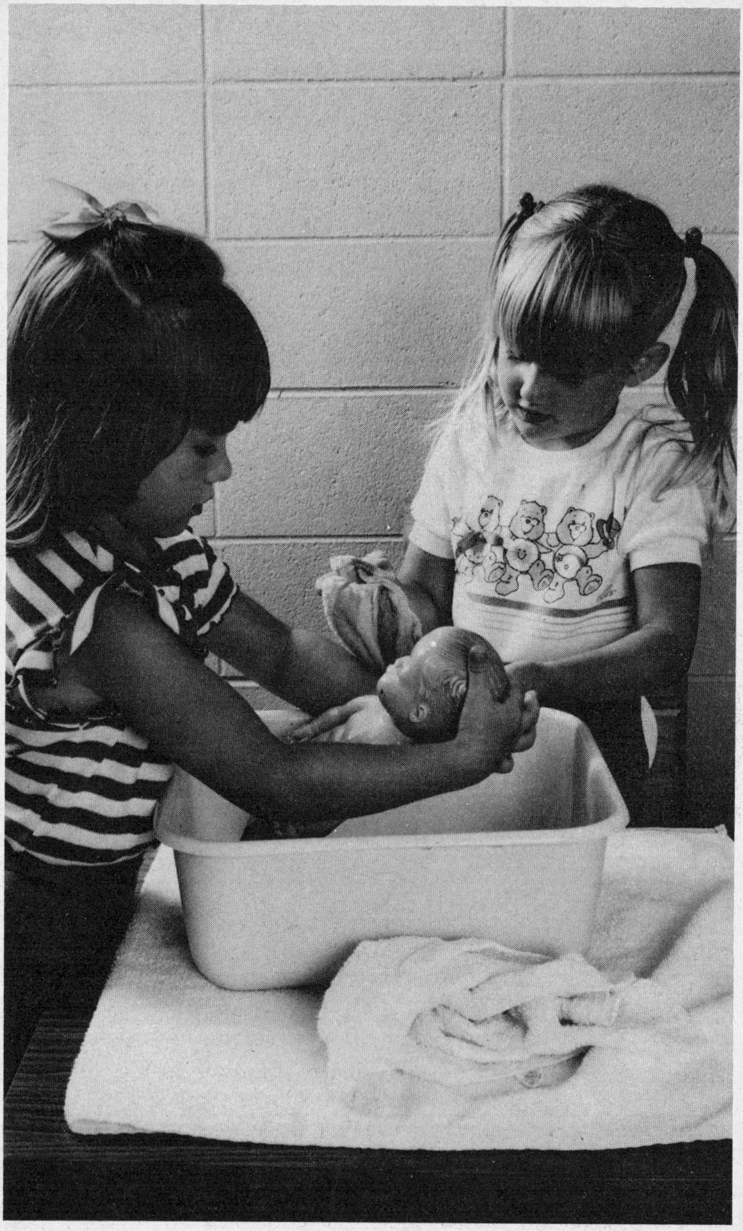

- The teacher can *follow through* with his assignments: collecting materials, room preparation, and personal study.
- The teacher can *share* in visiting and ministering to parents of preschoolers.
- The teacher can *fellowship* with other teachers so that they may support and minister to each other as well as work together.

After the teacher has studied the materials, attended the planning meeting, and gathered the necessary resources, one important task remains. This task is thought planning. All that has been discussed up to now is important and necessary. The teacher must now think through the Sunday session to be totally prepared to take advantage of opportunities to use interwoven, Bible-centered teaching.

- Think about the preschoolers in the department. Which ones may choose the activity for which you are responsible?
- Think about the materials you can provide and determine guidelines to share with the boys and girls.
- Think about the Bible teaching aim and how you can use your teaching time to accomplish this goal.
- Think about specific songs, Bible verses and thoughts, and conversation you can be ready to apply as the boys and girls work and play during the activities.
- Think about some ways you can initiate a prayer time or may sense a worship experience with one child or several.

Help for thought planning may be found in the teaching guide for the corresponding age group. The Bible teaching aim gives to teachers a purpose for the unit. It should be kept uppermost in the mind of the teacher throughout the month. All teaching suggestions for the month focus toward this aim. A list of Bible verses, Bible thoughts, and songs may be found at the beginning of each session. Guidance suggestions are made for each activity in each session in the teaching guides.

Planning and reviewing ways to use Bible verses, songs, and conversation enables the teacher to recall these as the session moves quickly or as pressures of details mount. For example, a teacher can get so involved in seeing that names are on pictures, clothes are covered with shirts, and hands are washed after painting that the opportunity to use a Bible verse or thought, to sing a song, or to sense a worship experience may slip away forever. If it has been thought about in advance, these important opportunities for teaching can be readily available to the teacher.

Resources for Planning
Many helps for planning are available for teachers. In addition to the Bible, the teaching guide is the teacher's most valuable resource. Usually the same person who writes the unit of study writes the planning suggestions. Therefore, planning details and resources suggested, as they come from the thoughts of the writer, are coordinated and significant to the session.

Teaching Guides
The suggestions in the teaching guides are carefully planned and thought through. However, there is one element of importance teachers must consider. These guides must be written for a large number of different kinds and sizes of churches to use. Writers of these materials do an excellent job, especially when one considers the wide spectrum of their audience. Curriculum writers cannot know your situation nor the preschoolers in your department. The guides do offer much specific help. *Preschool Bible Teacher A* has two sections. One is for teaching babies and creepers while the other section has suggestions for teaching toddlers. Guidance for teaching in Church Training is also offered. *Preschool Bible Teacher B* has a section written to help teachers of twos and a section written to help teachers of threes. There is also a special section for twos and threes in Church Training. *Preschool Bible Teacher C* is written for use with both fours and fives in Sunday School. It has a special section for teachers of fours and fives in Church Training. Bible Story Time materials are available for churches with combined age groupings (birth through twos, threes through fives, or birth through fives). Teaching suggestions for Sunday School and Church Training are in *Bible Story Time at Church*. Adapting the suggestions to meet the needs of preschoolers in your department is up to you. Choosing from the suggested activities you can provide is an important part of your planning.

There may be times when department teachers determine that a suggested activity is not appropriate for their situation. They may recall a previous learning experience they feel can help in reaching the Bible teaching aim. Teachers may wish to find a different experience to provide. Help in this area may be found in the book *How to Guide Preschoolers*. If a teacher is unsure of the activity he would like to provide, page 29 of the book offers guidelines in the selection of appropriate activities for preschoolers.

Activity Materials
Experimenting with actual materials to be used by preschoolers in the session can help teachers become more sensitive to guidelines to use with the boys and girls and to the experiences that may result. This also aids the teacher in determining whether the activity is too long or too involved for the age group.

Bible Background Help
In addition to specific help suggested by the writer of the lesson material, other resources may include Bible translations, commentaries, maps, and other kinds of books. These resources help teachers learn about the Bible background of the story to be used with the children. The more teachers learn about the subject, whether Bible story or preschoolers, the more excited and confident they become.

One Sunday afternoon a phone call came from a very competent preschool director. "Well, it happened just like you said it might," was the first statement I heard. "What happened?" I asked. She answered, "This morning, as I finished telling the story of Nehemiah rebuilding the wall, a child asked 'Just how did that wall get torn down in the first place?' I would have been able to answer if I had studied the Bible background," she added, pointing out her own shortcoming. We talked further and I thanked her for sharing this lesson with me. Her concluding statement was, "You can be sure that I will study the Bible background before telling a Bible story to preschoolers again."

Filmstrips
Showing a filmstrip during a weekly workers' meeting is a good variation. The filmstrip may be one for inspiration, it may be for training, or it may be one suggested for use with the children. If a filmstrip is to be used with the boys and girls on Sunday, the director and teachers will want to preview it if they have not seen it before. Consult the filmstrip guide for suggestions on showing the filmstrip.

Study Course Books
The age-group study course books can prove to be valuable resources as preschool teachers plan and questions arise. They may also be used in a brief training time during weekly workers' meetings.

Meeting with fellow Christians who share the same goal you have, to teach preschoolers in the department you have been assigned, is a worthwhile investment of your time. You know the individual needs of the boys and girls. You know the materials and resources available to you. You know what has already been accomplished in the department and you are working toward meeting needs of preschoolers in the department. Preschool teachers can inspire and stimulate each other as they come together for a common purpose. No, it is not a common purpose. It is God's purpose for the lives of preschoolers in your department.

---

[1] HOLY BIBLE *New International Version*, copyright © 1978, New York Bible Society. Used by permission. Subsequent quotations are marked NIV.
[2] This quotation is from the *Good News Bible*, the Bible in Today's English Version, Old Testament: Copyright © American Bible Society 1976; New Testament: Copyright © American Bible Society 1966, 1971, 1976. Used by permission.
[3] Willa Ruth Garlow, (printed narration), *Reach Out to Preschoolers*. (Nashville: Broadman Films, 1980), p. 5.
[4] Sue Raley, (printed narration), *Planning for Effective Teaching of Preschoolers*. (Nashville: Broadman Films, 1982), p. 4.

Chapter 5
Reaching Preschoolers to Teach

Reaching is . . .
  sending a postcard to a child.
  visiting in a home.
  making a phone call.
  making an announcement to an adult department.
  writing an article for the church paper.
  planning a special program for parents.
  enjoying a conversation in the supermarket.
  taking a pie to a new family.
  delivering a copy of *Beginning, Living, Growing, Bible Story Time at Home,* or *Bible Stories for Me.*
  participating in a "prospect search."
  inviting people with whom you work to church.
  placing a note in a baby's diaper bag.
  visiting someone in the hospital.

THEY CANNOT COME, THEY MUST BE BROUGHT

The attendance of preschoolers at your church depends on their parents, grandparents, other adults, and on you. The young child is dependent on parents or other caregivers to make decisions as to where he can go and activities in which he can participate. Preschool teachers have an important *CALLING, RESPONSIBILITY, OBLIGATION, TASK,* and *MINISTRY* to encourage parents to bring their preschoolers to the church for the various programs provided there. Young parents are more receptive to a visit from someone interested in their child than any other group a teacher visits for the church. Most parents in today's world are aware of ways boys and girls can be taught. They want to know what their child can learn at church. They are interested in the facilities provided for preschoolers. They are concerned about health and safety precautions.

Providing Space and Organization

The church has a responsibility to provide the best organizational structure and adequate space for preschoolers that is possible. However, this does not relieve the teacher of this responsibility. You, too, are the church. What will you do?

1. Accept and follow through on responsibilities assigned to you.
   IF this happened on the part of every teacher and leader in a church, the church could be the most successful organization in the world.
2. Support your pastor, other staff members, and others in leadership roles.
   IF this happened, every age group would be represented at weekly workers' meeting, in other organizational meetings, and on outreach night, resulting in a team effort that could "win the world" (at least your town) to Christ.
3. See that the department in which you work is one to which parents of preschoolers are excited about bringing their children.
   IF this happened, toys would be disinfected, shelves and other areas uncluttered, pictures on the eye level of the age group, and teachers would be in the room before the first child arrived.

The book *Basic Preschool Work* can help churches and teachers in determining the necessary structure for organizing preschool age groups. This book also suggests dimensions, equipment, and furnishings of rooms for preschoolers. Your room conveys a message to both parents and children. It says: "Welcome, we are ready for you," or _____

_____

(Complete each statement with an opposite statement.)

"Hello, this room is planned with you in mind," or _____

_____

"Come in, you will be secure and as physically safe as possible," or _____

_____

"Come back next week. This church cares about preschoolers,"

or _____

_____

What does your room say?

Promotion of Goals and Programs
It is important that information about the Preschool Division of the church be promoted. We know that what teachers are and do is one of the strongest influences in promoting the importance of the Preschool Division. However, people are responsive to young children and like to hear how their church is ministering to this age group. The most important group to whom you will want to promote goals and programs will be parents of preschoolers. The most effective way of reaching this group is through personal visiting in each home. Whether delivering the child's home book or a copy of *Living with Preschoolers,* or just dropping by information about the church and what is available for preschoolers and their parents can be shared.

Goal Sharing—Goals for the preschool years, for a unit of study, or for your next session may be shared with parents and other adults. This can be done through announcements, posters, letters, bulletin boards, and special meetings. Preschool Resource Kits often include posters for the door of the department. These posters inform parents about the emphasis for study for the month. A picture (from teaching picture sets) and your own printing can be used on the door or nearby in a similar way.

Parent-Worker Meetings are one of the most effective ways of reaching parents with special information. These meetings can be in many forms. A special speaker (child specialist, your pastor, a doctor) may be the feature. The meeting may be advertised as a working meeting for parents and teachers to work together to make the preschool rooms more attractive, cleaner, or to make equipment or teaching materials. The meeting may be one providing parents with the opportunity to experiment with materials and supplies used in teaching preschoolers. A book and toy fair before Christmas is a welcomed help to inexperienced parents and to doting grandparents. Plan the meeting well, regardless of the kind you have. Involve parents and teachers in the plans when possible. Appointing the following committees

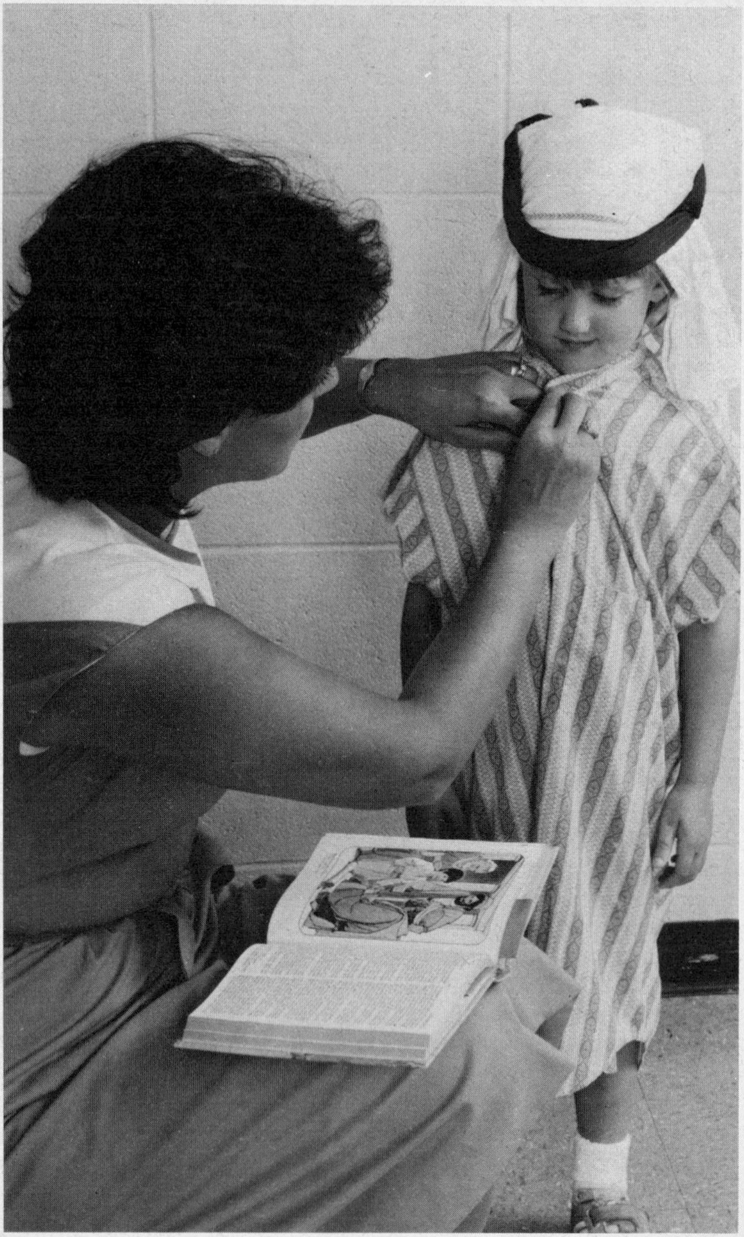

may help the planning: Program, Food, Publicity, Decorations, and Child-Care. Make it as meaningful as possible in as short a length of time as possible. Then, you can count on those attending being ready to participate in other meetings you plan.

Printed Material such as church newspapers or newsletters, personal letters or cards, or a Preschool Policies handbook are some ways of communicating through the printed word. These articles and statements need to share clearly the goals and the programs you wish to promote.

A Preschool Committee can help in areas of promotion. This committee can keep the work and needs of the Preschool Division before other organizational leadership and before the church. Members from this group or teachers from the Preschool Division may, occasionally, ask for a few minutes to speak in an adult department assembly time. This provides an opportunity to share goals and programs and to encourage participation in important ways such as the extended sessions.

A Positive Attitude on the part of each teacher in the Preschool Division may be your greatest asset for promotion. Be knowledgeable in what you are doing and in what you hope to accomplish. Know that your room reflects an attitude. Make it one you wish to convey. Accept the gifts and weaknesses of fellow teachers, of preschoolers, and of yourself. Feel good about your church. Share the good and forget about little things that irritate and bother. Remember that these things happen because we are all human. Be happy. Smile often. God has given you the best job in the church. Tell people about it!

Outreach—Ministry—Witnessing

Jesus said, "Ye are the light of the world . . . Let your light so shine before men, that they may see your good works, and glorify your Father which is in heaven" (Matt. 5:14-16). "It is the demonstrative Christian life still that raises the question in the unsaved: What shall I do with my life?" said Dr. Travis Berry, pastor of First Baptist Church, Plano, Texas.[1] He then told a story of a man to whom he and others had witnessed and had won to the Lord. This man, however, in his public commitment to Christ told those present that he was grateful for their witness, but that they had not won him to Christ. He told how his nephew, then thirteen, had for six years come each week to invite him to go to church. The man had never gone and the boy had never given up asking. It was his concern for his uncle and his persistence in his Christian task that had led this man to Christ. Christians may have difficulty realizing that the way they witness best is through their own lives. This may be said another way: "What you do speaks so loudly, I can't hear what you say." Regardless of how it is said, the truth remains—Christian, you are a witness to those with whom you come in contact. Preschool teachers, you are witnesses to preschoolers and their parents. You may be their strongest Christian influence.

As previously stated in this chapter, young parents are receptive to those who are interested in their child. Preschool teachers have the opportunity to cultivate a relationship with parents that can open up ministry and witnessing opportunities that may be difficult for others to discover.

Visiting

Visiting in the homes of preschoolers, whether enrolled in your department or prospects, can be an exciting experience. This experience may begin as a frightening one for a new teacher or an inexperienced visitor. Perhaps a few basic suggestions stated below can be helpful.

1. Plan a time to visit. Pray about the visits you will make.
2. Decide whether to call in advance. If the distance you will go is great, the more economical approach may be to make an appointment.
3. Be prepared to suggest an alternate date while you have the parent on the phone. They may not be available at your suggested time.
4. Take something with you: a church brochure, a copy of the child's home book *(Beginning, Living, Growing, Bible Stories for Me, Bible Story Time at Home)*, or a copy of *Living with Preschoolers*.
5. Try to know in advance: name(s) of the child(ren), approximate age of parents, and church affiliation, if any. This information is not necessary, but it is helpful.
6. Prepare for questions you may be asked such as:
   "What is your church membership?"
   "How old is your church?"
   "Where would each of my children go?"
   "Where would my husband and I go?"
   Know about your church. Locate adult departments and know names of adult teachers when possible.

7. Practice what you will say. Be honest and pleasant as you are greeted. Give your name, the name of your church, and why you have come. ("Hello, Mrs. Jones? My name is Susan Brown. I'm from Springdale Baptist Church and I have come to visit with you and your preschooler.")
8. Be prepared for a few unpleasant encounters. After all, did not Jesus experience a few of these during his ministry on earth?
9. Leave with some additional information: know names and ages of children and of parents. Gain information about the church affiliation of parents.
10. Follow up on your visit. Make a later call expressing your appreciation for the warm hospitality. Call to determine a location where you can meet the family on Sunday as they come to your church. Share information about parents with adult department teachers.

These are basic suggestions. Add others from your own experiences to the list. Visiting is a basic task of teachers. Use your own common sense, be natural, be yourself, and you may discover many enjoyable and lasting experiences as you visit preschoolers and their parents.

Witnessing

Witnessing, perhaps, is the most difficult of all tasks for the preschool teacher. Telling a lost man or woman what Christ means in your life is the best method of witnessing you can use. Your own personal testimony can be more impressive than any suggested plan you may ever follow. You need to use Scriptures to reinforce the importance of what you are saying. Teachers not totally familiar with where to locate these may wish to mark several in their personal Bible. There may be a time when you do not have access to a Bible. Having several verses printed on a card that you may carry in a pocket or purse may be an encouragement to you. The following Scriptures and subjects are suggested to help you formulate your own witnessing plan:

1. All have sinned: Romans 3:10, Romans 3:23
2. The results of sin; and God's answer: Romans 6:23, Galatians 6:7-8, John 3:16
3. What a person must do to be saved: Acts 3:19, Acts 16:31, Luke 12:8-9, Romans 10:9 Prayer and salvation: Romans 10:9, 10, 13
4. Baptism: Romans 6:4, Matthew 3:13-17

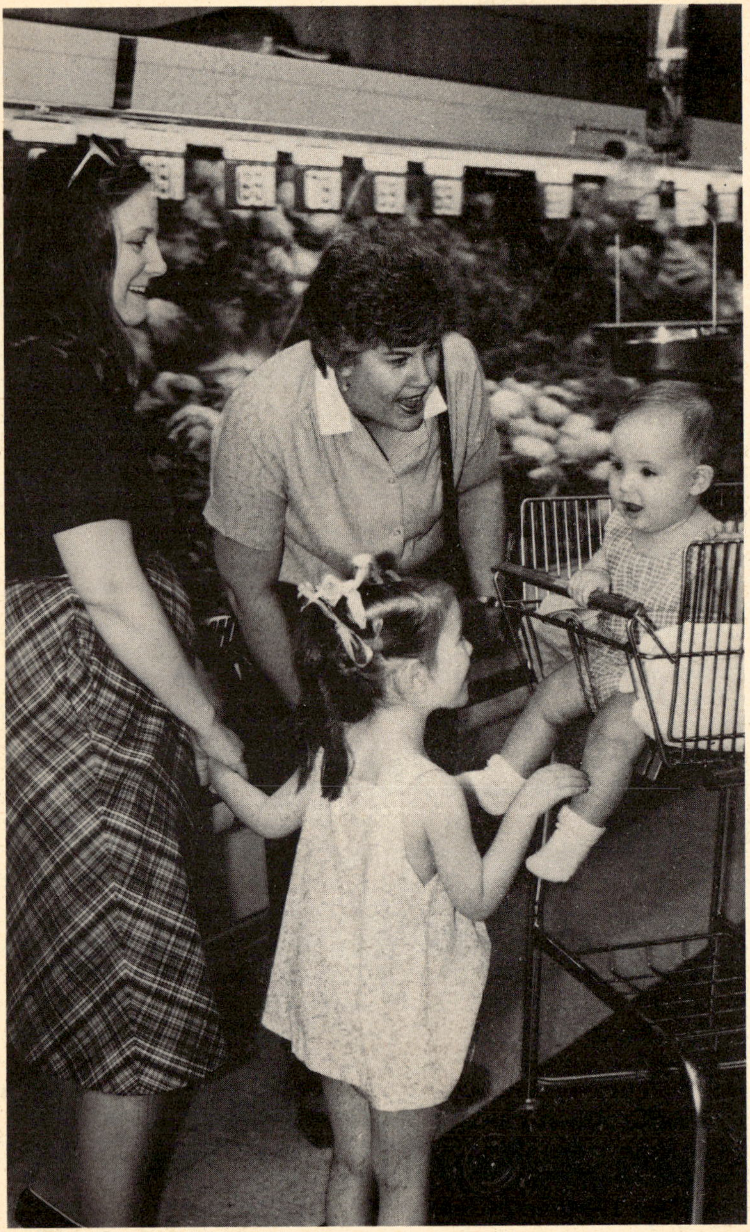

Many other Scriptures are available on these subjects. You may want to use those that are meaningful to you or that have been helpful in your own life. Because one of our goals is "a Christian home for every preschooler," we must be ready to witness. Do not overlook your greatest asset. Read Matthew 28:19-20. Pay close attention to the last statement and remember that you are not alone. Ask God to guide your words and feel confident that he will do so.

Ministering
Ministry opportunities are revealed to those who visit regularly. Many people have problems and needs. Because she has shown an interest in the child and his family, the preschool teacher may be the tie between a family and the church. You may be God's representative to a family.

The teacher needs to be alert to opportunities to be of service and to minister. Being there and helping during times of stress and need is an important means of reaching families for Christ and for the church. Teachers may find themselves in a situation too difficult to handle. If so, the pastor or other professional help may be of assistance. Most often, however, the situation will be such that a teacher can help. Watch for practical ways to minister. Asking if there is anything one can do usually receives a polite "No, thank you." Suggesting a specific action such as "Mrs. Adams, I am free tomorrow. I will drive you to the doctor," may solve a seemingly insurmountable problem for a young mother.

"Therefore, as we have opportunity, let us do good to all people, especially to those who belong to the family of believers" (Gal. 6:10, NIV).

Cradle Roll = Visitation is the title of a book, but it is also a very successful formula. The purpose of the Cradle Roll is to reach and bring into the Sunday School unenlisted children under two years of age. Cradle Roll can be one of the Preschool Division's most effective tools for outreach. You may have been asked or may already be a visitor-teacher in a Cradle Roll department. You know how important and helpful this department can be in reaching families for the church.

The Cradle Roll department is important enough that an entire book has been written to help workers with their specific assignment. *Cradle Roll = Visitation* is a guide for developing, organizing, and following through with a Cradle Roll department. *Cradle Roll = Visitation* is not a book for Cradle Roll teachers only. It is a book that all preschool teachers can benefit from reading. This book has many suggestions to help in visiting, witnessing, and ministering. It can be especially beneficial to teachers in churches with no Cradle Roll department. After reading this book, hopefully, the church devoid of a Cradle Roll will no longer be without this important means of outreach.

---

[1]Conversation with Dr. Travis Berry. Used by permission.

Chapter 6
Opportunities for Teaching Preschoolers the Bible

"Love the Lord your God with all your heart and with all your soul and with all your strength. These commandments that I give you today are to be upon your hearts. Impress them on your children. Talk about them when you sit at home and when you walk along the road, when you lie down and when you get up" (Deut. 6:5-7 NIV).

Moses gave the above instructions to the children of Israel following his reading of the Ten Commandments given to him by God. These words have a tone of urgency even today. When the opportunity is there, teach your children about the love of God and teach them to keep his commandments. There is concern, and there should be, that one hour a week may be the only Bible teaching many in the church receive. What about all the times the preschooler is at church?

Sunday School
Sunday School is the hour designated for Bible study. Usually, this is the hour with the greatest number of preschoolers present, therefore it is a most important time to provide and to plan to use in the best possible way. This hour undergirds and supports the morning worship service and much of the financing of a church. More adults, as well as preschoolers, are reached during this hour than at any other time. More visitors and prospects attend this organization than attend any other in most churches.

Adults come together during the Sunday School hour to read and study the Bible. Many of them have already studied their lesson material. They have used other study helps. They have interpreted for themselves and can share with each other what the Bible is saying to them.

Preschoolers come to Sunday School to learn Bible truths. They come at the age when there is more potential for learning than at any other age. This learning is dependent on the teacher in the preschool room. The preschooler needs the Scriptures interpreted to him just as the adult may use his Bible translation, commentary, or dictionary to help him. The preschool teacher translates Bible teachings to preschoolers as she applies the thought in the Scripture to the action or experience of the child.

Some parents, because of their background, may bring their preschooler only to Sunday School. This may be the one opportunity to teach some boys and girls. The Sunday School time is important. The Sunday School teacher has an important task of helping preschoolers learn Bible truths. That responsibility does not end when Sunday School concludes; it only begins.

Extended Session
The extended session is an extension of the Sunday School or the Church Training time. Taking advantage of a second hour to teach and to reinforce the Bible teaching of the first hour is a treasure other age-group teachers do not have. Because of the relationship of this hour to the Sunday School or Church Training Sessions, it is desirable to have a carry-over of teachers in the department. It is suggested that teachers teaching in the first hour take turns staying through the extended session to guide the work of the second hour. Volunteers outside the department are usually used as extended session teachers. These teachers need to be a part of the planning meeting and to be aware of preschoolers' needs, their characteristics, and ways of learning. They need the good example that trained teachers can set for them.

Organizing for the extended session is covered in chapter 7 of *Basic Preschool Work*. A separate packet of literature is available to help teachers with planning this time. The title of these pieces for specific age groups are *Extended Session for Babies and Toddlers, Extended Session for 2's and 3's,* and *Extended Session for 4's and 5's.*

Another important factor to consider about the extended session is that some preschoolers attend church only when their parents attend the worship service. This time, then, becomes the only opportunity for providing Bible learning activities to meet the needs of the child's inquisitive mind and active body. This can be a most rewarding hour for the teacher as he sees fruitful learning result whether in the form of an infant fed and sleeping

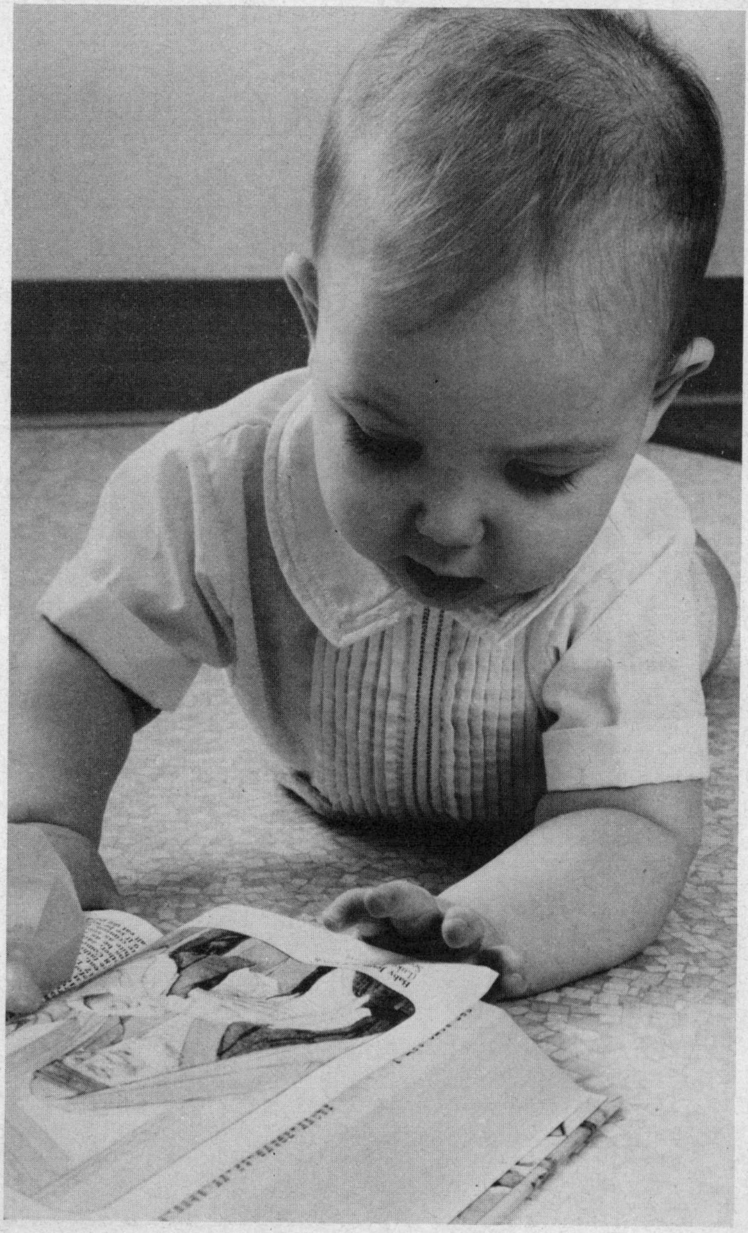

peacefully in a crib, or a two-year-old singing "I like to go to church."[1]

Parents, too, are responsive to the hour of planned teaching for their preschooler. Being able to attend the worship service knowing their child is receiving something constructive is rewarding for them and allows them to enjoy the worship service even more. Serving during the extended session is a genuine ministry to preschoolers and to their parents. Most important of all, it is another opportunity to guide young children in learning about God's love.

Church Training

The Church Training time most often precedes the evening worship service. The same teaching methods are used in this hour as are suggested for the Sunday School and extended session times and for anytime the preschooler is in his room at church. Specific teaching helps are available in the same literature piece that is ordered for Sunday School.

The new teacher benefits from knowing that both Sunday School and Church Training focus on the same subject (scope) area. The Bible teaching aims are different and a variety of activities and materials are suggested. Twos, threes, fours, and fives usually hear a different story in Church Training from what they heard during Sunday School. Preschool departments using *Bible Story Time at Church* repeat the Bible story.

Training for church membership is the primary goal of the Church Training hour. Providing appropriate kinds of foundational learning experiences for preschoolers is an opportunity a church cannot afford to miss. Even in these very early years, teachers are leading preschoolers to feel that church is important and that God wants them to be there and to be involved. What an important foundation for future church members!

Preschool Choir and Mission Friends

Preschool Choir and Mission Friends are two other church program organizations for preschoolers. Both of these organizations have specific goals for preschoolers. Both organizations have literature to aid in teaching. One has only to open the pages of these teaching guides to note that suggested methods of using the Bible are similar to those of the Sunday School and Church Training literature, as are the materials and basic approach to teaching. Obviously, each of these organizations has a specific task; however, they join other organizations in the overall task of teaching and reaching families.

Fortunate indeed are the preschoolers who are exposed to good teaching in all church program organizations. They can receive a strong foundation for future church membership and service as a Christian through teachers who understand their needs and how they learn.

To provide experiences helpful in forming Christian concepts through musical activities is an overall goal of the preschool choir program for fours and fives. (This program is not suggested for preschoolers younger than four.) To help preschoolers in developing positive attitudes toward music and in music appreciation are among other goals of the organization.

A teacher in Preschool choir may bring a collection of leaves for the children to examine. As the boys and girls look at the leaves, conversation may include God's plan for trees to shed their leaves in the fall and to have new ones in the spring. The teacher may lead the boys and girls to sing the song "Our World"[2] and to say thank you to God for beautiful leaves. The children may enjoy a further musical experience as they hold a leaf in each hand, moving hands high and low responding to a musical sound.

The teacher of Preschool choir for four- and five-year-olds can find many helpful suggestions in *The Music Leader. Music Time* is a leaflet printed for preschoolers to take home after each session.

Teaching the Bible in Mission Friends may be done as the three-year-olds are encouraged to take turns painting and the teacher sings the song "You Take Your Turn."[3] Bible learning may take place as children hear stories of a missionary in Korea, Africa, or Texas who uses the Bible to teach the people there about God.

Start, the teaching guide for preschoolers in Mission Friends, includes many suggestions for using the Bible with preschoolers. Bible thoughts and verses, and Bible stories are a part of each unit of study. The methods and materials used in Mission Friends are the same as in other organizations meeting the needs of preschoolers.

Vacation Bible School
Vacation Bible School is the most important special program a church may have for preschoolers. Usually provided in the summer, it attracts many boys and girls who do not attend the regular

organizations of the church. Helping boys and girls learn from the Bible is the basic goal. Reaching new families for the church and providing preschoolers with enjoyable experiences associated with church are other important goals.

Teachers in the other preschool organizations are needed and encouraged to work in Vacation Bible School. Preschool teachers have knowledge, information, and expertise that has been gained through experience and training. This can be shared with new and inexperienced teachers who are agreeable to teaching in Vacation Bible School. Knowing someone in the department is an experienced preschool teacher provides a secure feeling for the new teacher.

Vacation Bible School provides teachers the opportunity of concentrated Bible teaching. This program reaches outside the church membership and into the community. Many families have been added to church rolls through this important program. Teachers have major responsibilities as they study, plan, and teach in Vacation Bible School. As teachers in Vacation Bible School contact and visit the homes of preschoolers enrolled in the school, they almost always receive a warm welcome and a word of appreciation. Theirs may be the special privilege of enrolling a family in Bible study or encouraging them to begin regular attendance at church.

Each preschool teacher in the church, unless providentially hindered, should place Vacation Bible School on his or her calendar and consider it a privilege as well as a responsibility.

Weekday Early Education

The Church Weekday Early Education program encompasses a variety of ways of reaching preschoolers and their families. This program may be a half-day or extended day program. It may be a Mother's Day Out planned for one or two days a week. Many Southern Baptist churches have some type of ongoing weekday early education ministry. Meeting needs and reaching people are two of the main goals of a weekday program.

A church weekday early education program should be a part of the total church program. Church members may need help in seeing the potential for outreach and ministry in a weekday program for preschoolers. This vision can be encouraged by the teachers in the program. Increased learning from the Bible can result when preschoolers are reached and in attendance at the church.

Regretfully, some churches provide places for preschoolers to receive custodial care and nothing more. This is an unfortunate use of money, space, teaching abilities, and (most important of all) the child's most important years for growth and development. The difference is in the overall goals of a program and, ultimately, in the teachers. Child Development Center is the term used by some programs, especially those motivated by goals such as helping each child reach his full potential.

The Church Administration Department of The Sunday School Board has published teaching guides for every preschool age group in a weekday program. These guides are written by experienced preschool teachers and take into account the basic factors of child development as well as the opportunity to encourage moral and spiritual development in preschoolers.

Teachers in a weekday program can help and encourage preschoolers to grow as God planned, to learn about his world, and to relate happy experiences at church to Jesus, their best friend. Teachers in a program providing extended or all day care for preschoolers may have the child for more waking hours than his parents have him. No church or teacher wants to waste these precious times.

Throughout each day the child is present, many natural opportunities can occur or can be planned to allow a teacher to use Bible thoughts and truths with preschoolers in her class. It is very important that preschoolers are helped to make practical application of Bible truths. Whether involved in a game about numbers or learning about sounds, preschoolers can be led to an awareness of God's gift of eyes and ears and to his plan for them to learn. As younger preschoolers learn to trust the caregivers provided for them in the weekday program, they develop a good concept that church is a happy, secure, loving place to come.

Mother's Day Out (or Parent's Day Out) is a one- or two-day a week program very popular with mothers. Many churches provide this program allowing mothers of young children to leave their preschoolers in a secure, Christian environment while they attend to shopping, a doctor appointment, or have a little time for themselves. This can be a very worthy ministry of a church. If and when it is planned well, Mothers' Day Out not only is a welcome ministry to mothers but it is an anticipated day at the church for preschoolers. The *Mothers' Day Out Program Guide* by Kay Henry is a book to help teachers in planning for worthwhile learning experiences for preschoolers. This book has

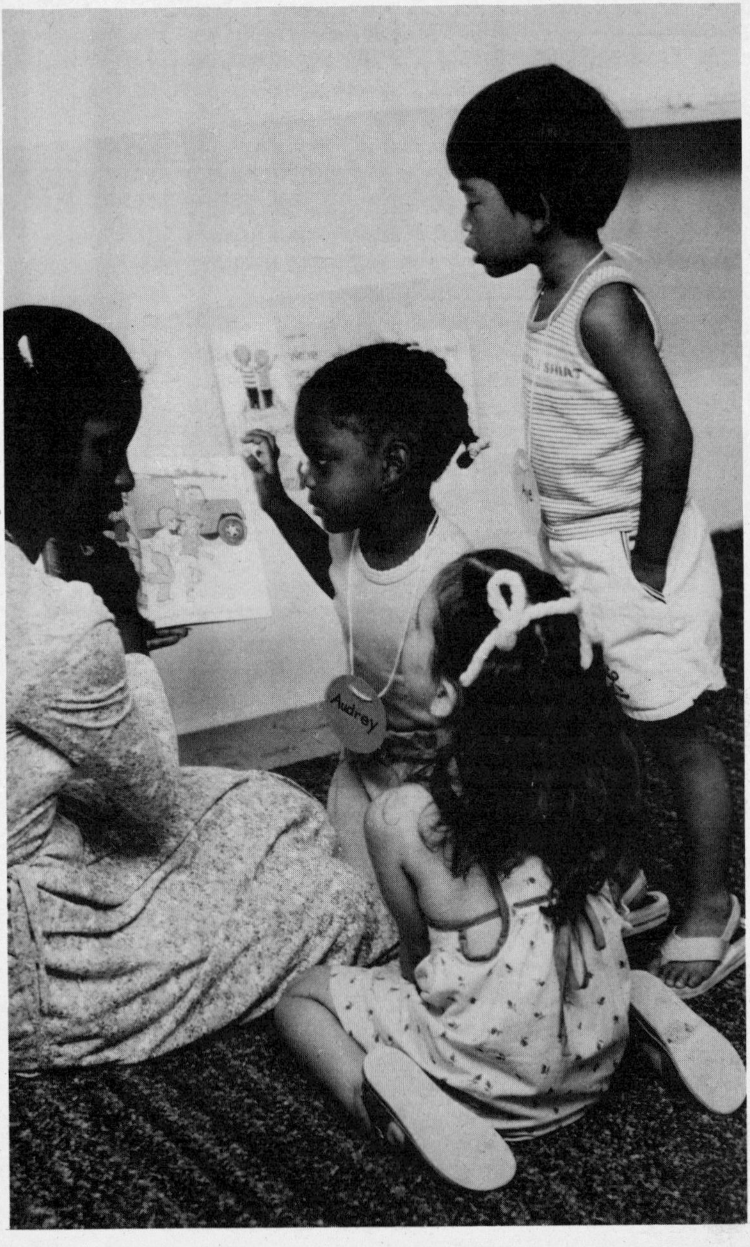
Audrey

units of study and schedule suggestions that are very similar to other programs for preschoolers.

In some ways, like Vacation Bible School, the church weekday program provides teachers with another opportunity to reach children not reached through other church programs. Therefore, taking advantage of this time to teach preschoolers biblical truths is a very worthwhile task.

Special Events
Study Courses and other times at church, such as adult fellowships, and other adult meetings make up a large portion of the younger preschoolers' time at church. Hopefully, no church is providing "baby-sitters" for these children. Because of the number of hours it may be necessary for some churches to employ special teachers to serve in younger preschool departments. These people are teachers, whether they plan to be or not. Preschoolers learn constantly and from everyone with whom they come in contact. Teachers of preschoolers, regardless of the child's age or the purpose of his being at church, should be trained and should have activities planned. The preschooler does not discern between the times he comes to church. He does not think to himself, "Today I am at church because it is Sunday and I am supposed to learn," or "Today I am at church so that my mother can attend a committee meeting, and I am not supposed to learn." Preschoolers are constantly learning, whether negative or positive. Some may be learning facts and developing spiritual concepts. Some may be learning that coming to church is not always a happy time for me.

Dedicated teachers at church want to be prepared to help the child learn from the Bible each time he comes to church. Undated units of study are available to help teachers in planning for additional times preschoolers are at church. Other help may be found in using suggestions from outdated literature. Preschool workers are wise to save several copies of outdated Vacation Bible School curriculum for use in planning special learning experiences. More suggestions than can possibly be used in the Bible school are always given in this material. An economical use of the material will be to use it a second time.

Having fun at church, and enjoying being there, is a very important learning experience. Young children feel secure when someone is in control. Allowing them to choose toys and materials to use and to play freely is good. An alert teacher nearby to guide and direct, to occasionally comfort, and to meet other needs, is necessary if desirable learning is to take place.

The *purpose* of this chapter has been:
1. To acquaint preschool teachers, and others interested in preschoolers, with the numbers of opportunities available for teaching boys and girls from the Bible.
2. To point out that preschoolers learn each time they come to church.
3. To emphasize the importance of planned learning activities each time preschoolers are in their room.
4. To remind preschool teachers that the same methods of teaching and kinds of materials are to be used each time preschoolers come to church.

As I think of the times preschoolers are at church, I am reminded of a passage of Scripture with which we are all familiar. "So, naturally, we proclaim Christ! We warn everyone we meet, and we teach everyone we can, all that we know about him, so that, if possible, we may bring every man up to his full maturity in Christ Jesus. This is what I am working at all the time with all the strength that God gives me" (Col. 1:28-29, Phillips).[4]

---

[1] Tune "I Like to Go to Church." *More Songs for 4's & 5's*, p. 70.
[2] Tune "Our World." *More Songs for 4's & 5's*, p. 57.
[3] Tune "You Take Your Turn." *Songs for the Young Child*, p. 85.
[4] Reprinted with permission of Macmillan Publishing Co., Inc. from J. B. Phillips: *The New Testament in Modern English,* Revised Edition. © J. B. Phillips 1958, 1960, 1972. Subsequent quotations are marked Phillips.

Chapter 7
Working with Others

The Home
The fact has long been established that every child is greatly affected by his heredity and environment. The child has individual characteristics and needs that are a result of these two influences. Everything that young child sees, hears, and does is filtered through the effects his heredity and environment have had on him. Our world is changing in many ways. However, one factor has not changed: The home continues to have by far the greatest influence on the child. Throughout the Bible, God emphasizes the parent-child relationship. The child benefits the most as parents and teachers work together to guide him to develop mentally, physically, emotionally, socially, and spiritually.

I Am a Teacher, What Can I Do?
Chapter 5 in this book has been devoted to the importance of visiting, witnessing, and ministering to those in the homes of preschoolers. There is no way that anything can take the place of a visit to the home of a preschooler and his family. Through visiting, teachers may discover needs in a family. Through visiting, teachers may develop a spirit of cooperation between themselves and parents as both share a mutual interest in the total development of the child.

Several years ago I read a statement that made a deep impression on me. In effect, the statement emphasized that preschool teachers may be the most qualified preschool authority known to parents of the children they teach. This places an additional reason for the preschool teacher to be as well trained and knowledgeable as he or she can be. This statement also makes it more important that preschool teachers make themselves more available to parents of preschoolers.

Preschool teachers can share observations and insights into young children with parents. A mother of a sixteen-month-old child talked nervously during a visit by one of the teachers from the child's Sunday School department. Sensing a hidden problem, the teacher succeeded in helping the mother feel secure enough to share her concern. The child, the mother felt, had developed a very negative feeling about the church. The mother said, "I know the teachers care for Emily. But I just wonder if she has had a bad experience in her room. She begins to cry when we start toward her room." The teacher was able to assure the mother that the action that concerned her was normal for a child of this age. The teacher also suggested a book she had that would help the mother, and she emphasized the importance of consistency in the child's attendance at church. This conversation prompted a second visit to the home to take a copy of *Understanding Today's Preschoolers,* and opened some opportunities for cooperation between the teachers and the home of Emily.

Preschool teachers can share knowledge and teaching methods they use to guide preschoolers with parents. Hearing the reasoning behind giving children choices and encouraging them to finish tasks can be helpful to young parents. A mother whose petite little girl brings home unidentifiable, and sometimes messy, art can be helped as she learns that the child is interested in the process involved rather than in the finished product in the use of art materials. To further hear how her child is developing a good self-concept as she carries our her own thoughts and plans in the use of these materials can encourage parents to provide similar opportunities in the home.

COMMUNICATION   CONSIDERATION

COORDINATION   CONCERN

CORRELATION   COOPERATION

CONVERSATION   CONSISTENCY

Three surprised parents stood at the door of a Church Training department for fours and fives. "How did you manage that?" one asked. "He never works that hard at home," exclaimed another parent. The teacher explained that the boys had worked very hard to build a church. They were so pleased with the structure that the teacher had suggested they leave it for all the boys and girls to see during the group-time experience. Now the boys were stacking the blocks back on the shelf in preparation for those who would use the room next, the teacher further explained to these parents.

Preschool teachers can help parents of preschoolers in guiding the child's spiritual development. In conversation with a parent, a preschool teacher was asked why their church did not have a "Children's Church." The teacher explained about the extended session. She explained that no one knows when the best time for young children to begin to attend the worship service occurs. She also shared that all information points to the learning that takes place in the lives of preschoolers. The teacher concluded by sharing the church's wish for four- and five-year-olds to attend the worship service with their parents. She included the influence of seeing their parents in prayer and worship and the importance of feeling a part of the church in worship as positive aspects of worship service attendance for older preschoolers.

Chapter 5 has already directed our thoughts to sharing goals with parents. As teachers and parents of preschoolers join together to help preschoolers reach their fullest potential—a common goal for both parents and teachers—the child will grow in ways pleasing to God, and families may be drawn closer to the church fellowship and to Christ.

Teachers and Fellow-Teachers
Developing good working relationships with other teachers in the same department is necessary. Communication between teachers of different organizations who use the same room and teach the same children is desirable. The results of teachers working together may include:
1. A healthy attitude that the room is for the children and does not belong to any one organization.
2. A wise use of money in the purchasing of small equipment and teaching materials.
3. A room arrangement that is more acceptable to all those using the room.

4. A continuity of teaching methods and guidelines to avoid confusion for the preschool boys and girls in the room for more than one session.
5. A more organized and efficient room as a result of cooperation and planning.
6. Better experiences for preschoolers who are in the room during study courses, revivals, or other special activities.
7. An attitude of cooperation, understanding, and support among those working with preschoolers in different organizations.
8. Encouragement for those teaching in each organization to leave the room ready for those in the next organization to use the room.
9. Training sessions planned for and attended by all preschool teachers.
10. A balanced distribution of teachers in all organizations.

The above results can probably be best accomplished by getting the preschool teachers in the various organizations together for a time of planning and discussion. The above list also may serve as a suggested list of discussion points if such a meeting occurs. The initial meeting can be called by the department director, the Preschool Division director, the pastor, the minister of education, or the minister of childhood education.

As preschool teachers in the various organizations in a church seek to provide the best in Bible teaching for each child, there will be no place for locked cabinets or hurt feelings. Decisions will be based on what is best for the child and a spirit of Christian love and consideration will be demonstrated before preschoolers and fellow teachers.

Preschool teachers can minister to each other. One of the greatest obstacles of enlistment of new teachers is the need for fellowship and support many feel they receive from their adult Sunday School class. Certainly, they should receive this from their class members. However, preschool teachers can receive the same fellowship and support from others with whom they work. Warm feelings and close ties develop as preschool teachers pray together and pray for each other.

To conclude the planning meeting, the director asked for prayer requests. Betty responded by saying, "I really need your prayers." She went on to share a serious family problem with fellow teachers in whom she trusted. The other teachers mentioned special prayer needs, and the three joined together in prayer. The director said at a later time that this was the beginning of a warm fellowship in their department that had not been experienced before.

Preschool teachers need to be ready to minister to one another. At least two teachers are suggested for a preschool department. Regardless of the number of teachers in a department, they can provide the fellowship and support to each other that is a need of most adults. This fellowship and encouragement from fellow Christians is one of the many rewards of being a Christian. This support includes ministry. A preschool teacher and her family were called out of town due to the unexpected death of a family member. When they returned, they found teachers from the preschool department where the mother taught had prepared a meal for the first evening, and had placed necessary food in the refrigerator for the next morning. This was a simple act of ministry, but it made the entire family of this preschool teacher feel cared for and loved in a special way. Relationships can be developed and strengthened as Christians perform acts of kindness for each other and for people outside the church.

Teachers and Church Staff
Whether the church in which you serve has one staff member or several staff members, working with these people is an important factor in teaching preschoolers, as well as in the total work of the church. The organization and staff assignments of the church in which you serve will determine the staff member to whom you relate in your specific teaching role.

The one-staff church means that the pastor is trying to be all things to all people. He is trying to be spiritual leader, educational advisor, and probably business administrator. He needs your help and support. Help him in these ways:
1. Work with other preschool teachers to find answers to as many of your questions as you can before involving him.
2. Keep him informed of the plans as well as the needs of the department in which you serve.
3. Make a list of your literature needs or changes for him or for whomever orders literature for the church.
4. Find a convenient time when you can share with your pastor important goals and information about the department.
5. Take advantage of training opportunities in your city, association, or state.
6. Support the total church program.

Another staff member to whom teachers may relate is the minister of education. This person will have had specialized training in the field of education and will be more alert to needs and problems teachers may have. Remember that his job is relating to every age group. He, too, will need your help. Some ways you may work effectively with your minister of education are:
1. Keep him informed about the needs and plans of the department.
2. Attend meetings and training sessions.
3. Give to him, in writing, whatever you need him to do or remember.
4. Be aware of new materials and helps available to enhance your teaching.
5. Seek his advice in important matters relating to the work of the department.
6. Cooperate with the overall work of the organization in which you are teaching.

Large churches with multiple staff members may have a minister of children's work or of childhood education. This person will be especially trained in the area of preschool education and will have more understanding of a program for preschoolers. Remember that this person must relate to all organizations for preschoolers and perhaps to another age group as well. This person is especially interested in you and your work. This person is like other staff members in needing your support. This suggestion for relating to other staff members is applicable here as well. Some additional suggestions for helping this person as well as other staff members are:
1. Notify the director of the department or enlist a substitute when you must be absent.
2. Call someone at the church when there is a serious illness or other special need among those in the department in which you serve.
3. Volunteer to help at special times (Vacation Bible School, study courses, during revivals, and other special programs at the church) when you can.
4. Take your turn teaching in the extended session.
5. Remember that church staff decisions must be based on what is best for the entire church.
6. Last, but far from least, pray for each staff member.

Chapter 8
The Rewards of Teaching

The Spiritual Growth of the Teacher
The husband of a preschool teacher was the director of training in his church. The teachers in his department had developed a Bible quiz to give to new students to help them see that they needed more Bible study. The director challenged his wife by saying, "As long as you've been down there in that preschool department, you surely need more Bible study." The wife responded by admitting she could always use more Bible study, but that she, too, had Bible background material to study. However, she accepted the challenge and took the test. To the amazement of her husband, this preschool teacher answered most of the questions right! Preschool teachers can be as knowledgeable about the Bible as they choose to be.

Studying the Bible and praying are the foundation of a Christian's growth. The dedicated preschool teacher will have realized the necessity of these areas in his or her life, and will have already made them a part of daily living. A Bible background summary of each Bible story for preschoolers is written for teachers in the age group teaching guides. Teachers are encouraged to study this material for personal development and growth as well as in preparation for sharing the story with preschoolers. The teacher who is interested can do other kinds of individual study.

As preschool teachers meet together to plan, a review or sharing in the study of the Bible background is often a part of the meeting. The meeting may also include a prayer time. In this way, preschool teachers become prayer support for each other, for their church, and for their work in the church. Becoming actively involved in the work of the Preschool department, and supporting other programs of the church cannot help but enhance the spiritual development of the preschool teacher. As the preschool teacher studies, learns, visits, and ministers in the name of Christ and the church, she will grow as a Christian.

Seeing Evidences of Learning and Growth in Preschoolers

"I don't want to lose this group of preschoolers."

"Our preschoolers have learned so much this year."

"Seems like we have just gotten our twos to this stage. We don't want to let them go."

"The new ones coming in will seem so young compared to these we are losing."

Hearing these kinds of statements as promotion time nears each year is rewarding. They indicate to me that teachers know and evaluate their children and that they are doing a good job teaching or they could not see such a marked difference. Statements such as the above also indicate the relationships of Christian love and friendship that have developed between teachers and their pupils. Because these statements are made by those who continue to teach preschoolers, they further indicate a love and dedication to the task as well as an understanding of preschoolers and how quickly they change, develop, and learn. Knowing these teachers, they may feel the same about the next group promoted to their department.

To begin with the child where he is and to work toward specific outcomes for him in the time he is assigned to you is a part of the responsibility of preschool teachers. This requires some evaluation. Evaluation of the child means recalling where the child was at the beginning of the year mentally, physically, emotionally, socially, and spiritually. Obviously, some of these stages of growth are easier to determine than others. For instance, it is not difficult to see evidences of physical growth as a creeper has advanced from crawling to walking. However, of significant importance is the three-year-old who learns how to manipulate a pair of scissors.

Mental growth is recognizable as fours and fives participate in a game of Bible story recall. The director or teacher usually begins a story and a child completes the story. Most fours and fives participate well in this game. Two-year-olds identify pictures of Jesus and sing songs indicating ways they are learning mentally.

Emotional and social growth can be noted as young preschoolers move from playing alone to playing alongside another child, to playing with another child. As a baby smiles at his

105

teacher, social development is beginning. The sixteen-month-old who cries each time she is left by her parents usually can be helped to handle this parent separation emotion.

How does one measure spiritual growth in a preschooler? Teachers may watch for quiet moments when a child has been helped (usually by a thought from the teacher) to think about God's love and care or about Jesus, his special friend. Spiritual growth is seen in the five-year-old who ceases to use the memorized prayer he has been taught by someone outside the department and begins to pray in his own words.

These and many other evidences of learning and growth are a part of the abundance of rewards and the joy that comes from teaching preschoolers.

Perhaps the following questions will help preschool teachers determine if growth and learning have taken place in preschoolers:

1. Do preschoolers usually enter the room willingly?
2. Do the children show feelings of security and relaxation once they are in the room?
3. Does the baby show an indication that he happily recognizes the face of his teacher?
4. Do the boys and girls enter into an activity with excitement and anticipation?
5. Have preschoolers developed new identifiable skills while in the department? (Example: Increase in attention span for preschoolers two and one-half through five years of age.)
6. Have you observed evidences of Bible learning and application, such as sharing and taking turns?
7. Are there other actions indicating boys and girls are learning to respect the rights of others?
8. Do middle and older preschoolers participate in conversation, songs, and games during group time?
9. In evaluating each monthly unit, were most of the Bible teaching aims accomplished in the lives of most of the boys and girls?
10. Is there some sign of a child's increased feeling of self-worth in each preschooler?

Seven-year-old Elizabeth's mother called me to find a time when I could talk with Elizabeth. This child was beginning to ask serious questions about salvation and the mother was not sure how to help her. Elizabeth and I visited together asking and answering questions. Her statements about what she wanted to do with her life and her answers to questions were childlike and basic. They were very normal for her age level. Her understanding of God and Jesus was real and showed the progression of learning that had taken place in her life. As we talked, I was thrilled by the evidences of learning in this child who had grown up in our church. As we prayed together, I silently thanked God for teachers who had done their jobs well. Together, Elizabeth and I thanked God for her parents who had brought her to church and for her church who cared for her and for other boys and girls.

Elizabeth and I probably will visit together again. There are some ways in which she needs further help in understanding what the Bible is saying to her. I have told her that her decision to accept Jesus as her Savior cannot be made by her parents or by any other person. She now knows that God will help her know when she is ready to understand and follow his plan for her life. I do not know when this decision will be made. I do know that, in all probability, I will not be present, nor will most of the teachers she has had in her lifetime. I know also that each of us will be able to have a sense of joy for the part we have played in this experience. Why am I writing about a seven-year-old in a book for teachers of preschoolers? The answer is simple: the basic foundations for conversion and Christian growth are laid by preschool teachers in a child's most formative years. Elizabeth was a baby in a younger preschool department, she was a one-, two-, three-, four-, and five-year-old in each of those respective departments.

Preschool teachers may not be the person directly involved with leading a child to Christ, but their teaching has been a vital part of the stages of learning and spiritual growth in the lives of those they have taught. Preschool teachers should sense a feeling of joy and success each time a previous pupil accepts Christ as Savior. Knowing he has had a very important role in God's plan for each person to learn of his love and care is a reward for every preschool teacher.

The Joy of Working Together with God
Many Scriptures have been used throughout this book indicating God's plan for teaching children. The Scriptures leave no question as to whether the Bible is for children. In his word, again and again, God says that children shall be taught. Fortunate is

the person who has been chosen to reveal the biblical message to preschoolers. In her book *Called to Teach Children* Muriel F. Blackwell emphasizes that persons can be and are called to teach children. She says, "You and God are partners in a very special way—you both touch the lives of children."[1] Preschool teachers who know they are within God's will find peace and happiness, and joy and excitement in their responsibility. They have within them a desire to learn and to prepare for their calling because they recognize that they are "labourers together with God." Can there be a more important assignment than teaching a human being in his earliest years of life about the love of God?

There are many Bible stories I enjoy sharing with preschoolers. One of my favorites is found in Mark 10:13-16. To see the interest in the faces of boys and girls as they hear how Jesus, after rebuking those who wanted to send the children away, called the little children to him, is a genuine joy of teaching preschoolers. With a feeling of gratitude, I recall Benjamin's question as I went into the room of two-year-olds on a Sunday morning. "Do you know about Jesus?" he asked. "Yes," I said, "and I'm glad Mrs. Roberts is helping you know about him too." Can there be a more important assignment than teaching preschoolers about Jesus, their friend?

Certainly the reason for teaching preschoolers is not for any reward unless that reward is knowing that one is pleasing God. God has placed preschoolers and their families in and near all our churches. His plan is for these children and their families to be reached with his word. God carries out that plan through his people. You and I are some of the people God has chosen. Preschoolers in your church and in mine are depending on us to help them learn from the Bible. God is depending on each of us to teach preschoolers in our church. My wish for each of us as we diligently seek to serve God, preschoolers and their families, is found in the book of Colossians. "We also pray that your outward lives, which men see, may bring credit to your master's name, and that you may bring joy to his heart by bearing genuine Christian fruit in all that you do, and that your knowledge of God may grow yet deeper" (Col. 1:10, Phillips).

---

[1] Muriel F. Blackwell, *Called to Teach Children*. (Nashville: Broadman Press, 1983), p. 99.

Personal Learning Activities

Chapter 1

1. In your own words, write what the Bible means to you.

_____

_____

_____

2. List other translations or books helpful to you as you personally study the Bible. _____

_____

_____

3. What is God's plan to help preschoolers learn from the Bible?

_____

_____

4. State your goal for teaching preschoolers.

_____

_____

_____

5. What do preschoolers learn before they begin to learn facts and information? _____

_____

6. List your favorite Scriptures about children.

_____

_____

_____

How have these Scriptures become meaningful to you?

_____

_____

Chapter 2

1. Think of a hobby, gift, or talent you have. Determine ways you can share this with preschoolers you teach or with their parents. _____

_____

2. Which of the "Responsibilities from God" is the most difficult for you? _____
List two ways you can overcome this difficulty.

_____

_____

3. Recall four necessary characteristics for a preschool teacher.

_____

_____

_____

4. Name three desirable characteristics for a preschool teacher.

_____

_____

_____

_____

_____

5. Think of the last teacher who resigned from your department. Ask yourself why this person resigned. What could have been done to encourage this teacher?

_____

_____

_____

Chapter 3

1. List five ways preschoolers learn.

_____

_____

2. Review the teaching guide from which you teach; locate an example of each method listed above.
3. List four methods suggested for enriching the preschooler's learning experiences during activity time.

_____

_____

_____

4. Determine which church study course book you plan to study next. Write the title. _____

_____
Commit yourself to a date to complete the reading of this book.

_____
5. Locate the scope (or subject) areas in the three units of your current teaching guide and record them.

_____

_____

6. Study the literature available for teaching the age group with which you work. Is there a suggested item you need to request? If so, record it below.

_____

_____

Chapter 4

1. List three results of an effective weekly workers' meeting.

_____

_____

_____

2. Review the "Suggestions for an Effective Workers' Meeting." As a teacher, determine which ones your participation in can be of most support to the director. Record those findings.

_____

_____

_____

3. Preschool department directors, evaluate your last weekly workers' meeting as you study the elements of a good planning meeting. Note two changes you may include in your next meeting. _____

_____

_____

4. List four ways teachers may enhance the effectiveness of the weekly workers' meeting.

_____

_____

5. Recall the last teaching session you attended. Where would additional thought planning have made your teaching more meaningful to the preschoolers?

6. Scan next month's unit of study. Note two activities preschool teachers will benefit from experimenting with during a weekly workers' meeting. Volunteer to collect these materials for one of your planning meetings. Record the two activities. _____

_____

Chapter 5

1. Complete the following statement in your own words. Reaching is _____

_____

2. List three things you can do to help in providing space and organization for the department in which you serve. _____

_____

_____

3. Evaluate your department from the viewpoint of a parent.
Does the room seem clean and uncluttered?
Are the teachers in the room before the first child arrives?
Are different pictures used in the room from time to time?
Are interesting learning materials attractively displayed to capture a child's attention?
Is the overall atmosphere warm, friendly, and loving?

4. In your own words, write your goal for teaching preschoolers.

_____

_____

_____

_____

5. Review the basic steps for visiting. You may have already ac-

complished all of these steps in your visiting. If not, which one

will you add as you make your next visit? _____
6. Think of a person you have had contact with recently to whom you feel the need to witness. Make a commitment about this concern.

Chapter 6

1 Make a list of the different times preschoolers come to your church building. Note the approximate teaching time beside

each of these attendance times. _____

_____

2. All of the times preschoolers are at church cannot be the responsibility of one teacher. However, better Bible teaching and worthwhile learning for preschoolers is the responsibility of each adult in the church. Ask yourself these questions as you consider the times preschoolers attend the church of which you are a member:
A. Are the rooms clean and prepared each time?

_____

B. Are planned learning activities being provided?

_____

_____

_____

3. What can you, as a teacher, do in your situation? Answering the following questions may be helpful:
A. How does your church provide workers for the extra times preschoolers are at church?
B. Is training provided for those who teach during special times at church?
C. How can I, as a Sunday School (Church Training) teacher, help others who teach preschoolers to receive training for their job?

4. Make a list of times preschoolers are at church, place beside each time a specific teaching guide available to help teachers plan for happier, more worthwhile times of learning at church.

_____

_____

5. Read Colossians 1:28-29, paying particular attention to Paul's concluding statement. Ask yourself, "What can I do to promote better Bible teaching for preschoolers each time they are at church?"

Chapter 7

1. Write in your own words the kind of relationship you think teachers should have with the parents of preschoolers in their

department. _____

_____

_____

2. List specific ways you have used your experiences with and observations of preschoolers to help parents.

_____

_____

3. Scan the "Results of Working Together" list. Determine those needed by preschool teachers in your church. Talk with your fellow workers to see if a general meeting can be planned, if this has not been done.
4. Ask yourself, "What can I do, individually, to be an example of Christian love, cooperation, and consideration as I strive to

teach preschoolers? _____

_____

5. To which church staff member do you relate in your teaching role? _____
How can you improve your relationship with this person?

_____

_____

_____

_____

Chapter 8

1. List two ways you have grown spiritually in the position you serve in your church.

_____

_____

2. Write below two opportunities for Christian growth and spiritual development you see through your work with preschoolers.

_____

_____

3. Choose a preschooler in your department, think back to when he came to your room. List one way that child has grown.

Mentally _____

Emotionally _____

Socially _____

Physically _____

Spiritually _____

4. Share with someone else your joy in teaching preschoolers. Write what you will say.

_____

_____

_____

_____

_____

5. What do you consider to be your greatest reward in teaching preschoolers? _____

_____

_____

_____

_____

_____

APPENDIX

BIBLE TEACHING TOOLS TO MAKE
The following are suggestions for different ages of preschoolers. Select those appropriate for the age groups you teach.

Bookmarks
Colorful and attractively made bookmarks may catch the attention of a child. Place these in the department Bible and in teachers' personal Bibles at verses you wish to emphasize.
- Cut bookmarks from different colors of construction paper. Select inexpensive stickers or small pictures from magazines, discarded greeting cards, wrapping paper, or back issues of the pupil's books.

- Cut bookmarks from grosgrain or satin ribbon in several colors.
- Make bookmarks with small nature items (leaves, flower petals, feathers, seed). Cover with clear contact paper or use a clear plastic film such as food wrap.
- Shave discarded crayons into small pieces. Press with a warm iron between two pieces of waxed paper. Cut into bookmark shapes.

- Prepare bookmarks from vinyl, a washable wall paper, or other washable materials for use in younger preschool departments.
- Start your own list of other ideas for bookmarks here:

_____

_____

_____

_____

Pictures

If a child cannot have a real experience, the next best way may be through vicarious experiences. A picture may remain in a child's mind much longer than words. Display pictures to clarify Bible truths.

- Cover pictures from *Preschool Pictures A, B,* or *C* with clear adhesive or contact paper. For younger preschoolers, it is desirable to glue pictures to poster board or corrugated cardboard before covering. This allows more usage as well as more durability.

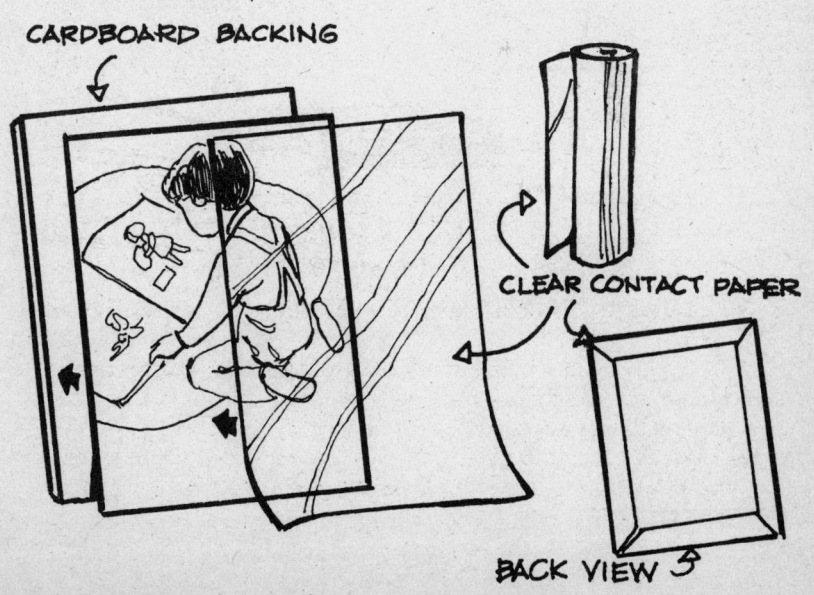

- Choose pictures from magazines, pupil's books, calendars, greeting cards, catalogs, and other sources. These may be used to create games as Bible markers, or as Bible related puzzles. To make a puzzle, glue pictures to poster board and cut into different shapes. Using a poster board or a large box top, draw around each piece with a heavy marker. Middle preschoolers especially enjoy placing pictures on the corresponding shape. Pictures of flowers, animals, food, Bible stories, people, and many others are usually plentiful. Choose those illustrating Bible truths you wish to convey.

- Make a nature puzzle. Locate duplicate pictures of six nature items. Glue one set of pictures on a quarter sheet (11 by 14 inch) of poster board. Mount the other set of pictures on small pieces of poster board.

Mark appropriate verses in the department Bible. As preschoolers match the pictures, a teacher may share the marked verses or she may ask the preschoolers to choose one of the markers for her to read the verse. Study the list in the back of this Appendix to help you determine appropriate Scriptures.

- Make stand-up picture boards that provide an attractive way to display different teaching pictures. Cut a piece of corrugated cardboard one inch larger than the size of the teaching pictures. Cover it with a colorful contact or adhesive paper, if desired. Make corners with corners cut from envelopes or use adhesive paper, making sure the front of the corners are open so that the corners of a picture slip in and out.

- Make mobiles with pictures from magazines, home books, or the resource kits. Hang these above cribs in younger preschool departments, and in eye-catching locations in middle and older preschool rooms. Select a colorful plastic hanger if only one hanger is desirable.

- Wire hangers may be used if two hangers are desired. Arrange one wire hanger at a right angle inside the other hanger. Twist the hook of one of the hangers to match the hook of the other. Wire or tie the hangers together at the hooks and in the lower center where they cross. Use heavy cord or wire ties made for use with bread or garbage sacks.

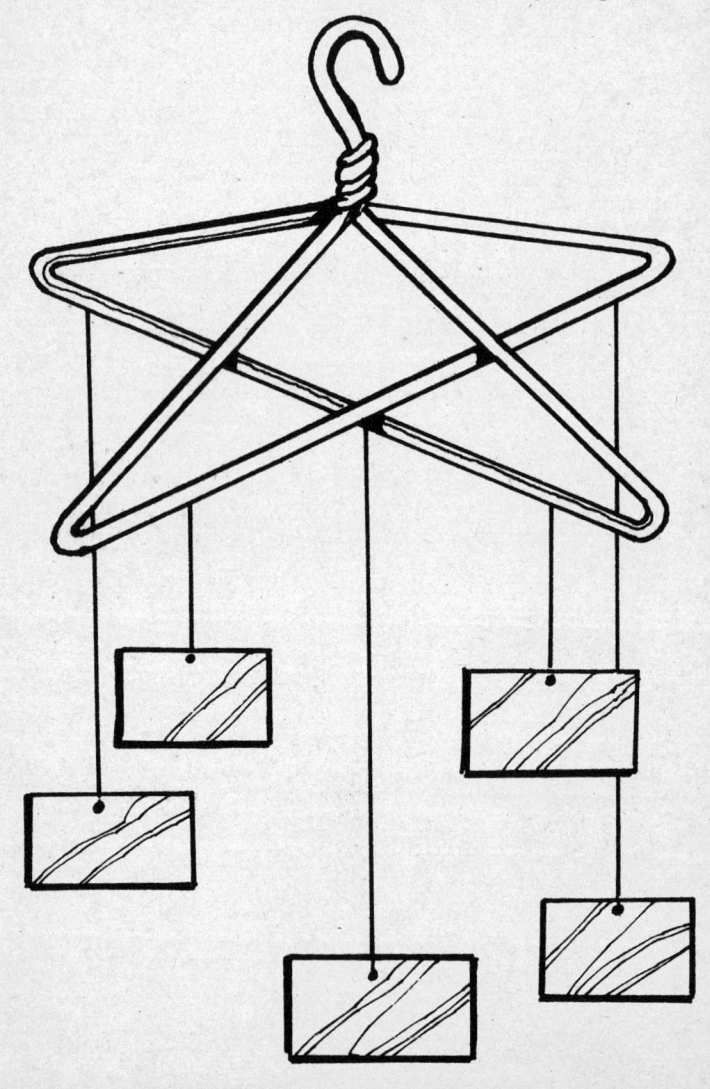

- Choose pictures from the home book, covering with a clear plastic (if desired) for a Bible activity. Glue back to back a picture of a Bible story and a current day picture. Place these in the department Bible at or near the correct reference to the story. Preschoolers enjoy turning through the Bible, locating the pictures, and talking about the story.

- Use pictures to make a song rebus or "picture song" for preschoolers. Songs such as "Tell Me That God Loves Me,"[1] "God Gave Me Eyes,"[2] and "God Who Made All Things"[3] are good songs to illustrate with pictures. Print words to the song on a sheet of poster board. Leave a blank space for words that can be illustrated with a picture. Glue or paste pictures where the words should be.

Tell Me That God Loves Me

Little 🕊 and 🌼 and 🌸
Tell me that God loves me.
☀ and ✨ and 📖 all three,
Tell me that God loves me.
🌙 and ⭐ at night I see,
Tell me that God loves me.

- Utilize this space to start your own list of other ideas for using pictures to help you teach preschoolers:

_____
_____
_____
_____

Games

Saying "Let's play a game" is an automatic attraction to a preschooler. Reading Bible verses, recalling an using Bible stories, recognizing Bible related pictures, as well as other uses of the Bible may be encouraged through the use of games. Worthwhile teaching is accomplished when preschoolers have happy experiences using the Bible.

"Guess the Color" Game

Make It

Make Bible markers with grosgrain or satin ribbon, using several colors. Tie smaller pieces of the ribbon onto a long cord or string. Space the pieces approximately 8 to 10 inches apart. Make a hole in the top of a coffee can or box. Cover the can with construction paper or colorful self-adhesive plastic. Place the string or cord with ribbon bows inside the container. Place the ribbon Bible markers at Bible verses related to the Bible teaching aims for the season.

Play It

Choose a child to pull the string until the first ribbon appears. Encourage the boys and girls to guess the color that comes out of the can as the string is pulled. Children may take turns pulling the string. Another preschooler may be chosen to locate the matching color of the marker in the Bible. The director or a teacher reads the verse.

"Choose the Picture" Game
Make It
Print Bible verses or thoughts on strips of construction paper or use Bible markers provided in the resource kits from time to time. Place the markers in the department Bible. Locate pictures that illustrate the Bible verses on the markers.
Play It
Place the pictures on the floor in front of the girls and boys. Ask a preschooler to choose a marker in the Bible. Read the verse. Ask another child to choose the picture that matches (illustrates) the verse.

"From This to That" Game
Make It
Locate magazine pictures of nature items such as sheep, trees, grain, cotton, and cows. Place these on separate rectangles of poster board or colored construction paper. Locate several smaller pictures of items that are made from the raw materials or animals in the first set of pictures. The smaller pictures may include dairy products, clothing (both cotton and wool), fruits, houses (and other items from wood), breads, macaroni, cereal, and other foods made from grain. Paste the smaller pictures on poster board or construction paper and place in a box top. Mark appropriate verses in the Bible. These may include:

"God made the trees" (Gen. 2:9).
"God makes the grass grow for the cattle" (Ps. 104:14).
"God gives food to us" (Ps. 136:25).
"God loves us" (1 John 4:10).

Play It
Locate and read the verses that are marked as an introduction to the game. Ask a child to pass the box top to each child in the semicircle so that each preschooler may take one of the pictures. Place the larger pictures on the floor and suggest to the boys and girls that they guess from which one their picture is made. When they decide from which one their picture comes, suggest that they place their picture on the larger one. Recall the Bible truths read earlier as natural opportunities occur.

"Color Toss" Game
Make It
Glue four colors of construction paper to a sheet of poster board. Make a heavy black line to separate the colors. Make matching squares of color and matching markers for the Bible. (These items may be used for several game approaches.) Clip the color squares to pictures illustrating the verses or stories to be emphasized. Make a bean bag or locate a large button to use in playing the game.
Play It
Place the four-color game board on the floor and show boys and girls where they may stand to toss the bean bag or button. As the color is chosen by tossing the bag or button, the child may then locate the matching color on a picture. Talk about the story illustrated. Another way to play this game is to place the marker in the Bible, matching the color on the board to the Bible marker.

"Match the Story" Game
Make It
Locate Bible story pictures from discarded issues of the pupil's book. Select pictures of stories that are illustrated in the sets of teaching pictures (*Preschool Pictures B* or *Preschool Pictures C*) or that are from the resource kits. If desired, place markers in the department Bible at the Scripture reference to the story illustrated in each picture.

Play It
Place the large pictures on the floor in front of the preschoolers. Ask boys and girls to choose small pictures and locate the picture about "their story." Suggest they place the small picture with the large one. Utilize this time to recall the stories illustrated.

"Find the Book" Game
Make It

Locate several books related to verses you wish to emphasize in this game. Examples are:

God's Summer Gifts or *God's Winter Gifts*—"God has made summer and winter" (Ps. 74:17).

Where Are You, God?—"Look at the wonderful things God made" (Job 37:14).

My Jesus Book—"God loved us and sent his Son" (1 John 4:10).

Outdoors with Jesus—"God made the flowers" (Gen. 1:11).

God Made the Sea, the Sand, and Me—"God made me" (Ps. 139:14).

Place a marker at the related verse in the Bible. Place a marker, the same color, in the corresponding book. The books may be placed on the book rack, or in other areas about the room.

Play It

Ask a child to choose a marker in the Bible. Read the verse. Choose another preschooler to find a book with the same color marker in it. Talk about what the book says or show the pictures to the boys and girls. Read one of the books if time permits. Tell the girls and boys that these books will be on the book rack next Sunday for them to "read."

"Memory" Game
Make It
Scan past issues of the pupil's book or resource kit items and locate two identical pictures of the same Bible story, making five or six sets of two. Paste all the pictures on the same kind of paper (construction, poster board, or typing paper) to make them identical on the back. Place one set of pictures in the Bible at the Scripture reference to the story in the picture

Play It
Ask a child to choose a picture marker in the Bible. Involve the boys and girls in recalling the story. Place one set of pictures facedown on the floor, talking about which story is portrayed in the picture as you turn each one facedown. The preschoolers may take turns choosing pictures from the second set and placing them on the one they think is the matching picture on the floor.

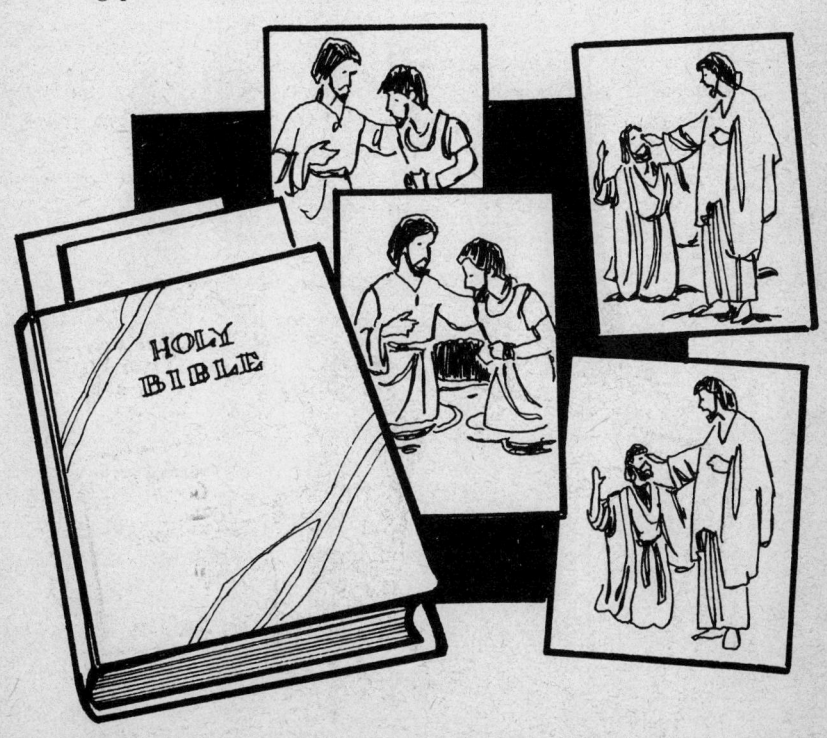

"Bible Story Toss" Game
Make It
From outdated issues of the pupil's book, locate pictures of nine Bible stories you wish to emphasize. Divide a sheet of poster board into nine equal blocks, drawing three across and three down. Glue a picture in the center of each block. Locate teaching pictures of each story. If desired, mark Scripture references to the stories in the department Bible.
Play It
Ask boys and girls to take turns tossing a bean bag (or large button) on the board to choose a story. Another child may point out the corresponding story from teaching pictures placed on the floor in front of the children. Locate references to one or two of the stories in the Bible. Discuss the characters or plot of the story as it is chosen.

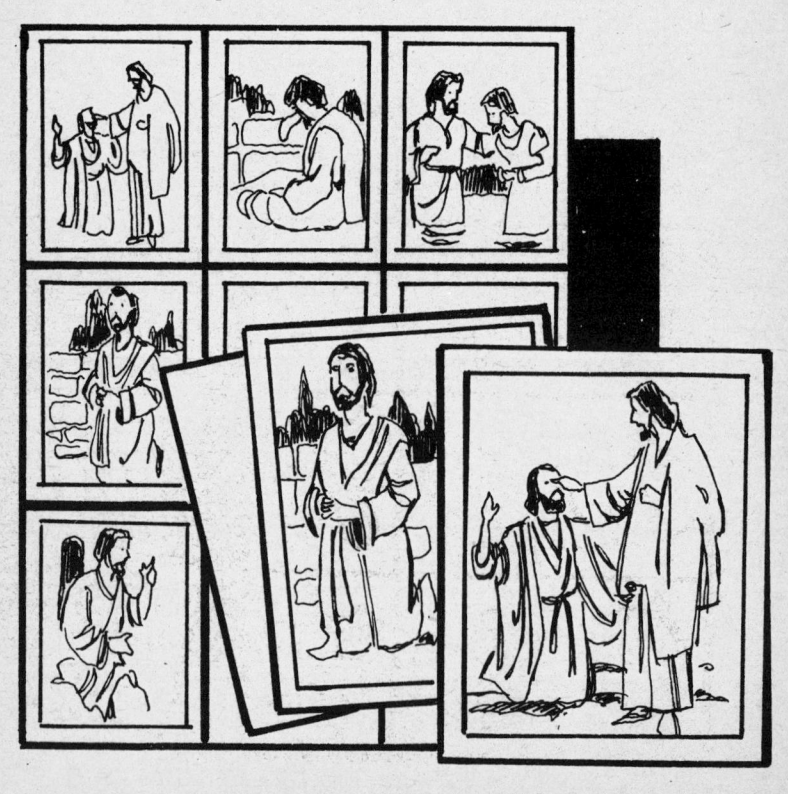

"Lotto" Game
Make It
Cut poster board into 7 by 9 inch pieces. Divide each piece into nine blocks with a broad, felt-tipped black marker. Purchase several books of inexpensive stickers such as butterflies, birds, shells, fall nuts and leaves, or other realistic nature materials. Make four game boards by gluing one sticker in each block on the poster board. Make small cards from poster board or cut file cards in half. These should be the size of the blocks on the game boards. Make book markers using the same stickers as used in the game. Mark appropriate verses. Read the chart in the back of this Appendix to help you locate the verses.

Play It
This game may be placed in the nature area and played by one to four preschoolers. Place the small cards, picture side down, in the center of the table or on the floor. The boys and girls take a card from the top of the stack, matching it to the picture on their game board. The game may continue until all the same cards are used. A teacher may suggest locating markers in the Bible with a sticker matching one on a child's card. Read the Bible thoughts as the game is played.

"Picture and Song" Game
Make It
Mark several of the songs in *More Songs for 4's & 5's* which contain Bible truths. Examples are:
   "Think of the Wonders," page 53
   "Love One Another," page 20
   "Children, Obey Your Parents," page 16
   "The Bible Tells Us Jesus Grew," page 27
   "Jesus Loves Me," page 41
   "God Wants Us to Be Kind," page 21
Select songs from *Songs for the Young Child* to play the game with three-year-olds. Locate pictures illustrating the Bible truth in each song.
Play It
Place the pictures on the picture rail or on the floor. Ask a child to choose one of the markers in the songbook. Sing the song. Ask another child to choose the picture he thinks illustrates the song.

A "Singing" Game
Make It
Place different colors of construction paper markers at verses in the Bible. Locate songs relating to the verses. Place markers in corresponding colors at the appropriate songs in the songbook. Examples using *Songs for the Young Child* are:
"God Loves Me," page 4; 1 John 4:10.
"The Stars Are in the Sky," page 6; Genesis 1:16.
"God Made the Flowers," page 8; Genesis 1:11.
"Jesus Loves Me," page 17; John 15:12.

Select songs from *More Songs for 4's & 5's* to play the game with four-and five-year-olds.

Another way to play this game with three-year-olds is to use the song "I Open My Bible,"[4] locating pictures of Jesus, David and the sheep, Samuel, birds, flowers, and leaves. Refer to the Bible truths at the end of this Appendix for suggested Scriptures.

Play It
Ask a child to choose a marker in the Bible. Read the verse. Ask another child to locate the same color marker in the songbook, stating that the song is about the verse you just read. Sing the song.

Guidelines in the use of games with preschoolers are:
1. Keep the game, especially the instructions, as simple and clear as possible.
2. There is never one winner in a game for preschoolers. They all win.

3. Be prepared to accept the child's choice in matching games. If clarification is needed, that is, a picture is chosen that does not match a verse, song, or color, conversation may help a child change her mind. Occasionally, the boys and girls may suggest the better one. Always avoid embarrassing a child in front of his peers.
4. Boys and girls learn through repetition and may ask to play a game over a second time.
5. Make games so that they may be kept for use at other times. Avoid using the same game too often.
6. Keep an extra game available to assure yourself of having enough planned for each group time. Do not be disappointed if there is not enough time to play a game. Save it for another time.
7. Prepare games, pictures, and markers to last. Mount items on stiff paper or poster board. Certain items may be made more durable by covering with clear contact plastic.
8. Store games for quick reference. Games and markers may be kept in appropriately marked file folders. Zipper-type plastic bags may be used to organize games and markers. Accordion folders (available from office supply stores) may offer a good way to organize Bible activity items. For larger items, place them in large gift boxes (shirt size) or clothing boxes from department stores.

---

[1] Tune "Tell Me That God Loves Me." *More Songs for 4's & 5's*, p. 45.
[2] Tune "God Gave Me Eyes." *More Songs for 4's & 5's*, p. 49.
[3] Tune "God Who Made All Things." *More Songs for 4's & 5's*, p. 48.
[4] Tune "I Open My Bible." *More Songs for 4's & 5's*, p. 64.

"Ideas for Bible Related Activities"

Games are an enjoyable way of learning from and using the Bible. Start your collection of games. Record those you especially like to use with preschoolers. Be creative. Think up some of your own. Copy down instructions of favorites from the preschool curriculum materials in the following space to help you build on your resources for Bible related activities. Use this space to begin your collection:

"Ideas for Bible Related Activities"

"Ideas for Bible Related Activities"

"Ideas for Bible Related Activities"

"Ideas for Bible Related Activities"

"Ideas for Bible Related Activities"

Bible Verses and Thoughts for Birth Through Five

Bible Thought	Reference	Age Designation*
Church		
"Be glad and sing happy songs."	Psalm 9:2	B C
"Be glad and sing praises."	Psalm 9:2	C
"Be kind to one another."	Ephesians 4:32	B C
"Bring an offering to church."	Malachi 3:10	C
"Bring an offering to thank God."	1 Chronicles 16:29	C
"Help one another."	Galatians 5:13	A B C
"I like to go to church."	Psalm 122:1	A B C
"I thank God."	2 Timothy 1:3	C
"I was glad when they said, 'Let us go to church.'"	Psalm 122:1	C
"I will praise God with a song."	Psalm 69:30	C
"I will sing to God."	Exodus 15:1	C
"It is a good thing to give thanks."	Psalm 92:1	C
"Jesus went to church."	Luke 4:16	A B C
"Love one another."	1 John 4:7	B C
"Let us love one another."	1 John 4:7	C
"Sing praises to God."	Psalm 47:6	C
"Sing thanks to God."	Psalm 147:7	C
"We are helpers."	2 Corinthians 1:24	A B C
"We give thanks to God."	Colossians 1:3	C
"We work together."	1 Corinthians 3:9	A B C

Bible Verses and Thoughts for Birth Through Five

Bible Thought	Reference	Age Designation*
Family		
"Be kind to one another."	Ephesians 4:32	B C
"Children, obey your parents."	Colossians 3:20	C
"Help one another."	Galatians 5:13	A B C
"Jesus' family went to church."	Luke 2:27	A B C
"Jesus loves you."	John 15:12	A B C
"Jesus went to church with his family."	Luke 2:27	A B C
"Let us love one another."	1 John 4:7	C
"Love one another."	1 John 4:7	B C
"Love your father and mother."	Exodus 20:12	C
"We are helpers."	2 Corinthians 1:24	A B C
"We work together."	1 Corinthians 3:9	A B C
God and Natural World		
"Everything God made is beautiful."	Ecclesiastes 3:11	C
"Give thanks to God.	Psalm 136:1	C
"God called the light day and the darkness he called night."	Genesis 1:5	C
"God cares for you."	1 Peter 5:7	C
"God gives food to animals."	Psalm 147:9	B C
"God gives food to birds."	Psalm 147:9	B C

Bible Verses and Thoughts for Birth Through Five

Bible Thought	Reference	Age Designation*
"God gives food to us."	Psalm 136:25	A B C
"God gives the moon and stars for a light by night."	Jeremiah 31:35	C
"God gives the sun for a light by day."	Jeremiah 31:35	C
"God gives us things to enjoy."	1 Timothy 6:17	C
"God has made the summer."	Psalm 74:17	B C
"God has made the winter."	Psalm 74:17	B C
"God is good to us."	Psalm 73:1	A B C
"God looked at everything he had made and he was very pleased."	Genesis 1:31	C
"God loves us."	1 John 4:10	A B C
"God loved us and sent his Son."	1 John 4:10	C
"God made all kinds of trees to grow."	Genesis 2:9	C
"God made animals."	Genesis 1:25	B C
"God made the birds."	Genesis 1:21	A B C
"God made the cattle."	Genesis 1:25	C
"God made the clouds."	Job 36:27	B C
"God made the cows."	Genesis 1:25	A B C

Bible Verses and Thoughts for Birth Through Five

Bible Thought	Reference	Age Designation*
"God made the fish."	Genesis 1:21	A B C
"God made the flowers."	Genesis 1:11	A B C
"God made the fruit."	Genesis 1:11	A B C
"God made the grass."	Genesis 1:11	A B C
"God made the grasshopper."	Amos 7:1	A B C
"God made me."	Psalm 139:14 or Psalm 119:73	B C
"God made the moon."	Genesis 1:16	A B C
"God made the moon and stars to shine in the night."	Jeremiah 31:35	B C
"God made the ocean and dry land."	Psalm 95:5	C
"God made people."	Genesis 1:27	A B C
"God made plants with seed."	Genesis 1:11	C
"God made the rain to fall."	Job 36:27	C
"God made the rivers."	Psalm 104:10	C
"God made the summer."	Psalm 74:17	B C
"God made the sun."	Genesis 1:16	A B C
"God made the sun, the moon, and the stars."	Jeremiah 31:35	B C
"God made the sun to shine in the day."	Jeremiah 31:35	B C

Bible Verses and Thoughts for Birth Through Five

Bible Thought	Reference	Age Designation*
"God made the stars."	Genesis 1:16	A B C
"God made the trees."	Genesis 2:9 or Genesis 1:11	A B C
"God made the water."	Psalm 104:10	A B C
"God made the winter."	Psalm 74:17	B C
"God made the world."	Acts 17:24	C
"God made clouds in the sky."	Psalm 147:8	C
"God makes darkness and it is night."	Psalm 104:20	C
"God makes his sun to rise."	Matthew 5:45	C
"God makes rain."	Psalm 147:8	A B C
"God makes the grass to grow."	Psalm 147:8 or Psalm 104:14	A B C
"God makes the grass grow for the cattle."	Psalm 104:14	C
"God makes the lightning flash."	Jeremiah 10:13	B C
"God makes the lightning flash with the rain."	Jeremiah 10:13	C
"God makes the wind to blow."	Psalm 147:18	C
"God sends the autumn rain."	Jeremiah 5:24	C
"God sends the frost."	Psalm 147:16	C
"God sends the rain."	Jeremiah 5:24	A B C
"God sends the spring rain."	Jeremiah 5:24	C

Bible Verses and Thoughts for Birth Through Five

Bible Thought	Reference	Age Designation*
"God sends the snow."	Psalm 147:16	B C
"I thank God."	2 Timothy 1:3	C
"I will praise God with a song."	Psalm 69:30	C
"I will sing to God."	Exodus 15:1	C
"It is a good thing to give thanks to God."	Psalm 92:1	C
"Look at the wonderful things God made."	Job 37:14	C
"Love God."	Mark 12:30	C
"Say thank you to God."	Psalm 136:1	B
"Sing praises to God."	Psalm 47:6	C
"Sing thanks to God."	Psalm 147:7	C
"Think about the wonderful things God made."	Job 37:14	C
"The birds have nests."	Matthew 8:20	C
"The birds make their nests."	Psalm 104:17	C
"The flowers grow."	Song of Solomon 2:12	A B
"The flowers grow and bloom."	Song of Solomon 2:12	C
"The moon shines in the night."	Psalm 136:9	A B C
"The stars shine in the night."	Psalm 136:9	A B C
"The sun shines in the day."	Psalm 136:8	C
"The time of the singing of birds is come."	Song of Solomon 2:12	C

Bible Verses and Thoughts for Birth Through Five

Bible Thought	Reference	Age Designation*
Jesus		
"God loves us and sent his son."	1 John 4:10	C
"Jesus grew."	Luke 2:52	A B C
"Jesus grew and became strong."	Luke 2:40	C
"Jesus grew tall."	Luke 2:52	A B C
"Jesus' family went to church."	Luke 2:27	A B C
"Jesus had friends."	Luke 2:52	A B C
"Jesus lived in Nazareth."	Matthew 2:23	C
"Jesus loves you."	John 15:12	A B C
"Jesus said, 'I love you.'"	John 15:9	A B C
"Jesus said, 'Let the children come to me.'"	Matthew 19:14	B C
"Jesus said, 'Love one another.'"	John 15:17	B C
"Jesus said, 'You are my friends.'"	John 15:14-15	A B C
"Jesus was born in Bethlehem."	Matthew 2:1	C
"Jesus went about doing good."	Acts 10:38	C
"Jesus went to church."	Luke 4:16 or Luke 2:27	A B C
"Jesus went to church with his family."	Luke 2:27	A B C
"Mary and Joseph took Jesus to church."	Luke 2:27	A B
Others		
"A friend loves at all times."	Proverbs 17:17	C

Bible Verses and Thoughts for Birth Through Five

Bible Thought	Reference	Age Designation*
"Be kind to one another."	Ephesians 4:23	B C
"God is good to us."	Psalm 73:1	A B C
"God made us."	Psalm 100:3	A B C
"Help one another."	Galatians 5:13	A B C
"Jesus had friends."	Luke 2:52	A B C
"Jesus said, 'Love one another.'"	John 15:17	A B C
"Jesus said, 'You are my friends.'"	John 15:14-15	A B C
"Let us love one another."	1 John 4:7	C
"Love one another."	1 John 4:7	B C
"We are helpers."	2 Corinthians 1:24	A B C
"We work together."	1 Corinthians 3:9	A B C

Self

Bible Thought	Reference	Age Designation*
"Be glad and sing happy songs."	Psalm 9:2	C
"Be glad and sing praises."	Psalm 9:2	C
"Be kind to one another."	Ephesians 4:32	B C
"Give thanks to God."	Psalm 136:1	C
"God cares for you."	1 Peter 5:7	C
"God gave us ears to hear."	Proverbs 20:12	A B C
"God gave us ears to hear and eyes to see."	Proverbs 20:12	C
"God gave us eyes to see."	Proverbs 20:12	C
"God gives food to us."	Psalm 136:25	A B C

Bible Verses and Thoughts for Birth Through Five

Bible Thought	Reference	Age Designation*
"God is good to us."	Psalm 73:1	A B C
"God loved us and sent his Son."	1 John 4:10	C
"God loves us."	1 John 4:10	A B C
"God made me."	Psalm 139:14	B C
"God made people."	Genesis 1:27	C
"God made us."	Psalm 100:3	A B C
"Help one another."	Galatians 5:13	A B C
"I am wonderfully made."	Psalm 139:14	C
"I like to go to church."	Psalm 122:1	A B C
"I thank God."	2 Timothy 1:3	C
"I was glad when they said, 'Let us go to church.'"	Psalm 122:1	C
"I will praise God with a song."	Psalm 69:30	C
"I will sing to God."	Exodus 15:1	C
"It is a good thing to give thanks to God."	Psalm 92:1	C
"Jesus loves you."	John 15:12	A B C
"Jesus said, 'I love you.'"	John 15:9	A B C
"Jesus said, 'You are my friends.'"	John 15:14-15	A B C
"Let us love one another."	1 John 4:7	C
"Love one another."	1 John 4:7	B C
"Love God."	Mark 12:30	C
"Say thank you to God."	Psalm 136:1	B
"Sing thanks to God."	Psalm 147:7	C

Bible Verses and Thoughts for Birth Through Five

Bible Thought	Reference	Age Designation*
"Sing praises to God."	Psalm 147:6	C
"We are helpers."	2 Corinthians 1:24	A B C
"We give thanks to God."	1 Corinthians 3:9	C
"We work together."	1 Corinthians 3:9	A B C
"Work with your hands."	1 Thessalonians 4:11	C

*A—birth through toddlers; B—twos and threes; C—fours and fives

Resources

Curriculum and Related Materials
Preschool Bible Teacher A
Preschool Bible Teacher A Resource Kit
Extended Session for Babies and Toddlers
Beginning
Preschool Bible Teacher B
Preschool Bible Teacher B Resource Kit
Extended Session for 2's & 3's
Living
Preschool Bible Teacher C
Preschool Bible Teacher C Resource Kit
Extended Session for 4's & 5's
Growing
Bible Story Time at Church
Bible Story Time at Church Resource Kit
Bible Story Time at Home
Bible Stories for Me
Look and Listen
Preschool Leadership
Living with Preschoolers
Home Life
Open Windows
Preschool Pictures A, Set 1
Preschool Pictures A, Set 2
Preschool Pictures A, Set 3
Preschool Pictures B, Set 1
Preschool Pictures B, Set 2
Preschool Pictures C, Set 1
Preschool Pictures C, Set 2
Preschool Pictures C, Set 3
Preschool Pictures C, Set 4

Weekday Resources
Mother's Day Out Program Guide
Mother's Day Out Program (filmstrip)
WEE LEARN Curriculum Guide for Two-Year-Olds
WEE LEARN for Two-Year-Olds
WEE LEARN Curriculum Guide for Four-Year-Olds
WEE LEARN for Four-Year-Olds
WEE LEARN Curriculum Guide for Five-Year-Olds

WEE LEARN for Five-Year-Olds
Church Weekday Early Education Teacher's Guide
Church Weekday Early Education Teaching Guide: Birth-Three
Moral and Spiritual Development for the Young Child, Rouse and Waldrop

Program Helps
Guidelines for Bible Study for Workers with Preschoolers and Children
Preschool and Children's Workers Witnessing
Your Child in the Sunday School
Make Your Own Preschool Furniture

Free Helps
Cradle Roll Sunday School Department Standard
Preschool Sunday School Department Standard
Responsibilities of Preschool Sunday School Workers
Responsibilities of Cradle Roll Workers
Visitation—Why and How
Preschool Division Director at Work
HomeReach
Winning Parents of Preschoolers to Christ
How a Preschooler Learns About God
Start A Cradle Roll and Grow
Literature Choices for Preschool Workers
Curriculum Materials for Preschool Teachers in Sunday School and Church Training
Cradle Roll Prospect Discovery Ideas
How to Use Preschool Curriculum Materials
Preschool Books and Supplies

Preschool Standard of Excellence
Steps to Church Training for Preschoolers
Duties and Responsibilities of Preschool Workers in Church Training

Undated Units
Birth-Threes
Animal Friends
God Loves My Family
God Loves My Family Resource Kit
God's Outdoors
Good Food to Eat
Jesus Loves Me
Love One Another
People at Church Love Me
People at Church Love Me Resource Kit
My Church

Four-Fives
God Planned for Families
God Planned for Families Resource Kit
Help One Another
How the Bible Helps People
Me, Music, Others
People at Church Learn About God and Jesus
People at Church Learn About God and Jesus Resource Kit
Playing and Singing Together
Things Families Do Together

Study Course Books
Sunday School and Church Training
Basic Preschool Work, Terrell
Basic Preschool Work Resource Kit
Bible Teaching for Preschoolers, Uland
Bible Teaching for Preschoolers Resource Kit
Cradle Roll = Visitation, Nelson
How to Guide Preschoolers, Strickland

How to Guide Preschoolers Resource Kit
Reaching Preschoolers, Strickland
Understanding Today's Preschoolers, Waldrop
Understanding Today's Preschoolers Resource Kit

Music Resources
Guiding Fours and Fives in Musical Experiences, Baker, Key, Butler
Music Time
Preschool Music Resource Kit
The Music Leader

Mission Friends
Mission Friends Leader Manual
Start
Share

Filmstrips
"How to Teach Preschoolers in Sunday School Series"
  Teaching Preschoolers Through Activities
  Understanding the Preschool Child
  You, A Teacher of Preschoolers
  Planning for Effective Teaching of Preschoolers
Using Bible Story Time Materials
Winning Parents of Preschoolers
Extended Session for Preschoolers
Reach Out to Preschoolers
Reach Out with Cradle Roll
Teaching Babies and Toddlers
Teaching Twos and Threes
Teaching Fours and Fives

Videos
Teaching Fours and Fives at Church
Teaching Babies, Creepers, and Toddlers at Church

Additional Resources
Read-to-Me Bible
Your Home and Christian Discipline (Equipping Center)
Equipping Teachers to Teach (Equipping Center)
Songs for the Young Child (Book and Recordings)
More Songs for 4's & 5's (Book and Recordings)

Sunday School, Church Training, and Music curriculum materials and Program Helps are available from Materials Services Department, 127 Ninth Avenue, North, Nashville, Tennessee 37234.

Mission Friends curriculum materials are available from Woman's Missionary Union, P.O. Box C-10, Birmingham, Alabama 35283-0010.

Free Helps are available from your state Sunday School or Church Training department office.

Weekday Resources, Undated Units, Study Course Books, Filmstrips, Videos, Equipping Centers, and *Read-to-Me Bible* are available from Baptist Book Stores.

The Church Study Course

The Church Study Course is a Southern Baptist education system consisting of short courses for adults and youth combined with a credit and recognition system. Also available in the system are noncredit short courses (called foundational units) for children and preschoolers. The course in the Church Study Course are for use in addition to the ongoing study and training curricula made available to churches by the denomination.

More than 500 courses are available in 23 subject areas. Courses are flexible enough to offer credit for either individual or group study. Credit is awarded for each course completed. These credits may be applied to one or more of the 100 plus diploma plans in the system. Diplomas are available for most leadership positions as well as general diplomas for all Christians. These diplomas are the certification that a person has completed from five to eight prescribed courses. Diploma requirements are given in the catalogs.

"Enrollment" in a diploma plan is made by completing Form 725 "Church Study Course Enrollment/Credit Request" and sending it to the Awards Office at the Sunday School Board. Course credit may also be requested on this form. A permanent record of courses and diplomas will be maintained by the Awards Office. Twice each year up-to-date reports called "transcripts" will be sent to churches to distribute to members participating in the Church Study Course. Each transcript will list courses and diplomas completed and will show progress toward diplomas currently being sought. The transcript will show which courses are needed to complete diploma requirements. A diploma will be issued automatically when the final requirement is met.

Complete details about the Church Study Course system, courses available, and diplomas offered may be found in a current copy of the *Church Study Course Catalog* and in the study course section of the *Church Materials Catalog*. Study course materials are available from Baptist Book Stores.

The Church Study Course system is simple enough to be administered by volunteer workers with limited time. The system is universal so that credit earned in one church is recognized in all other Southern Baptist churches. Approximately 500,000 awards are earned by adults and youth each year.

The Church Study Course is promoted by the Sunday School Board, 127 Ninth Avenue, North, Nashville, Tennessee 37234; by Woman's Missionary Union, P.O. Box C-10, Birmingham, Alabama 35283-0010; by the Brotherhood Commission, 1548 Poplar Avenue, Memphis, Tennessee 38104; and by the respective departments of the state conventions affiliated with the Southern Baptist Convention.

How to Request Credit for this Course
This book is the text for course number 13373 in subject area: "Sunday School Leadership." This course is designed for five hours of group study.

Credit for this course may be obtained in two ways:

1. Read the book and attend class sessions. (If you are absent from one or more sessions, complete the "Personal Learning Activities" for the material missed.)

2. Read the book and complete the "Personal Learning Activities." (Written work should be submitted to an appropriate church leader.)

A request for credit may be made on Form 725 "Church Study Course Enrollment/Credit Request" and sent to the Awards Office, Sunday School Board, 127 Ninth Avenue, North, Nashville, Tennessee 37234. The form on the following page may be used to request credit.

A record of your awards will be maintained by the Awards Office. Twice each year copies will be sent to churches for distribution to members.